CAN TECHNOLOGY HELPS BUSINESSES TO CREATE SALE CHANCE

JOHN LOK

Made with ♥ on the Notion Press Platform
www.notionpress.com

Our business society had developed long time from farming period to manufacturing period, then to service industry period, till to nowadays technology service and manufacturing period. It brings this question: Can technology or human behavior may influence economic development? Human ourselves foolish or enjoyment behavior whether which can bring economic recession? If human can forgive to do enjoyment behavior, we can help economic growth? I shall apply behavioral economic theory to indicate cases to attempt to explain these questions.

In our societies , any kinds of products or services must need to apply demand and supply economic theory to analyze whether the kind of product or service may be value to invent to sell or serve to their customers in consumer market, if the kind of product or service demand number is less, then it ought not to raise manufacturing number to avoid "low price " sale or if the kind of product demand number is more, then it ought raise manufacturing number to have enough number in order to raise " high price" sale to satisfy customers their needs to buy their products.However, whether your product or serive's demand number depends on supply number or your product or service's supply number depends on demand number in order to make ths sale price is reasonable high or low level and reasonable supply number valuation. In my this book, I shall indicate some actual product or service social suitation to explain whether these kinds of product or service is depended on either demand or supply aspect more in behavioral economic view. In my this book final chapter I shall indicate whether artifical intelligence can help businessmen to predict houselder consumption behavior? Can new technology helps future businesses to create sale chance ? I shall follow behavioral economic analysis theory to explain why and how future AI technology can influence householder electricity energy consumers to decide or choose how much electricity energy to feel that it is the most reasonable judgement of electricity energy consumption in their daily life.

Contents

Prologue

Contents

Robots take our jobs behavioral and economy influences
    Robot job behavior brings economy influences
p.75-90
    Intellectual human economic behaviors
What does intellectual human economic behaviors
mean ?
    The relationship between social change and human
behavior
    How human productive behavior may influence economic development

● New Zealand farmer individual wine productive behavior
● America high technological productive behavior
● China share market investing behavior
Why has any individual country have many people invest share behavior
which can influence the country's macro consumption desire?
Can technology influence human shopping behavioral change?
p.91-116
Why and how human behavior may influence the country's economic
growth or recession?
Technology how impacts human behavior changing?
How and why employees behaviors may influence economy development?
Robots invention whether they can help organizations to raise efficiencies
or inefficiencies?
Why social behavior may influence organizational strategy needs to be
changed ?
How and why human behavior may influence economic growth or
recession?
Reasons why human behavior may influence economic recession or growth
?
p.117-135
    Chapter 5 How (AI) technology impacts energy industry development
    House quality influences householder
electricity energy consumption behavior p.136-155
Environmental impacts of householder
greenhouse gas electricity energy
consumption activities p.156-166

The effect of house space occupancy
and building characteristics on
householder electricity energy use p.167-180

How to help low income houehold
earners to reduce not essential
electricity energy expenditure
spending at homes p.181-190

Factors influence householder energy
efficient consumption behaviors
at homes p.191-200

How artificial intelligence impacts energy
consumers using behaviours
    How to apply (AI) technology to improve
energy efficiency and better climate change
and the security of energy supply as well
a resource efficiency?

The relationship between consumer
psychology and behavior p.201-217

CHAPTER ONE

Explaining supply and demand economic theory relationship

The difference between past and nowadays economists their demand and supply economic theory explanation?

The law of supply and demand defines the relationship between the price of a given good or product and the willingness of people to either buy or sell it. Generally, as the price of a good increases, people are willing to supply more and demand less. These economists had explained economic demand and supply theory as below:

Philosopher John Locke is credited with one of the earliest written descriptions of this economic principle in his 1691 publication, Some Considerations of the Consequences of the Lowering of Interest and the Raising of the Value of Money. Locke addressed the concept of supply and demand as part of a discussion about interest rates in 17th-century England. Many merchants wanted the government to lower the cap on interest rates charged by private lenders so that people could borrow more money and thus purchase more goods. Locke argued that the free-market economy should set rates because government regulation could have unintended consequences. If the lending industry were left alone, interest rates would regulate themselves, Locke wrote: "The price of any commodity rises or falls by the proportion of the number of buyers and sellers."

Sir James Steuart's Inquiry into the Principles of Political Economy, published in 1796, was the first known printed use of the term "supply and demand." When Steuart wrote his treatise on political economy, one of his main concerns was the impact of supply and demand on laborers.

Adam Smith dealt extensively with the topic in his 1776 epic economic work, The Wealth of Nations. Often referred to as the Father of Economics, Smith explained the concept of supply and demand as an "invisible hand" that naturally guides the economy. According to Smith, the invisible hand is the automatic pricing and distribution mechanisms in the economy. Smith described a society in which bakers and butchers provide products that individuals need and want, providing a supply that meets demand and developing an economy that benefits everyone. It is important to note that Smith's ideas haven't gone without critique over the years since his ideas were first published, though. Over time, his ideas have been added to in order to represent the changing times and include concepts such as marginal utility, comparative advantage, entrepreneurship, the time-preference theory of interest, and monetary theory.

One of Marshall's most important contributions to microeconomics was his introduction of the concept of price elasticity of demand, which examines how price changes affect demand. In theory, people buy less of a particular product if the price increases, but Marshall noted that in real life, this behavior was not always true. The prices of some goods can increase without reducing demand, which means their prices are inelastic. Inelastic goods tend to include items such as medication or food that consumers deem crucial to daily life. Marshall argued that supply and demand, costs of production, and price elasticity all work together.

Nowadays economists they explain demand and supply economic theory, they have some different to past economists whose explanation as below:

How Does Supply and Demand Work? The law of supply and demand is a theory that explains the interaction between the sellers of a resource and the buyers of that resource. Generally, as price increases, people are willing to supply more and demand less and vice versa when the price falls. What does the bottom line mean. Despite the origins of the law of supply and demand beginning hundreds of years ago, it's still a topic frequently referenced and utilized today in economic theory and discussions. The theory has developed over time to accommodate recent technological and economical advancements, but the basic ideas of the theory remain largely the same.

Does demand depend on supply?

Supply and Demand Determine the Price of Goods and Quantities Produced and Consumed. Consumers may exhaust the available supply of a good by purchasing a given good or service at a high volume. This leads to an increase in demand. As demand increases, the available supply also decreases.

What does market demand depend on?

Market factors affecting demand of consumer goods. The demand for a good increases or decreases depending on several factors. This includes the product's price, perceived quality, advertising spend, consumer income, consumer confidence, and changes in taste and fashion.

Who controls the demand in supply and demand?

Supply and demand are in turn determined by technology and the conditions under which people operate. At one extreme, the market could be populated by a large number of virtually identical sellers and buyers (for example, the market for ballpoint pens).

What are the two laws of demand and supply?

The law of demand holds that the demand level for a product or a resource will decline as its price rises, and rise as the price drops. Conversely, the law of supply says higher prices boost supply of an economic good while lower ones tend to diminish it.

What factors affect demand and supply?

Price fluctuations are a strong factor affecting supply and demand. When a product gets expensive enough that the average consumer no longer feels it is worth it to buy the product, then the demand declines. This leads to cuts in production that will hopefully stabilize the product's value.

What factors affect demand and demand?

Demand may be defined as the quantity of a commodity that a consumer is able and willing to buy, at each possible price, over a given period of time. ● Essential elements of demand are quantity, ability, willingness, prices, and period of time.

Which factors affect supply?

Generally, the supply of a product depends on its price and other variables such as the cost of production.

a. Price. Price can be understood as what the consumer is willing to pay to receive a good or service. ...

b. Cost of production. ...

c. Technology. ...

d. Governments' policies. ...

e. Transportation condition.

How does supply and demand work together?

It's a fundamental economic principle that when supply exceeds demand for a good or service, prices fall. When demand exceeds supply, prices tend to rise. There is an inverse relationship between the supply and prices of goods and services when demand is unchanged.

What happens to supply when demand increases?

An increase in demand, all other things unchanged, will cause the equilibrium price to rise; quantity supplied will increase. A decrease in demand will cause the equilibrium price to fall; quantity supplied will decrease.

What is the theory of demand?

Demand theory describes the way that changes in the quantity of a good or service demanded by consumers affects its price in the market, The theory states that the higher the price of a product is, all else equal, the less of it will be demanded, inferring a downward sloping demand curve.

What are the 4 basic laws of supply and demand?

1) If the supply increases and demand stays the same, the price will go down. 2) If the supply decreases and demand stays the same, the price will go up. 3) If the supply stays the same and demand increases, the price will go up. 4) If the supply stays the same and demand decreases, the price will go down.

The different types of demand are as follows:

i. Individual and Market Demand: ...

ii. Organization and Industry Demand: ...

iii. Autonomous and Derived Demand: ...

iv. Demand for Perishable and Durable Goods: ...

v. Short-term and Long-term Demand:

What creates demand for a product?

You can create demand for a unique product if you can manage to solve a persistent problem for the consumer. People are always running away from pain, and providing them with an outlet is a sure-fire way to create massive demand for your goods.

What are the 7 factors that affect supply?

The seven factors which affect the changes of supply are as follows: (i) Natural Conditions (ii) Technical Progress (iii) Change in Factor Prices (iv) Transport Improvements (v) Calamities (vi) Monopolies (vii) Fiscal Policy.

What can affect demand?

Factors Affecting Demand

    Price of the Product. ...

The Consumer's Income. ...

The Price of Related Goods. ...
The Tastes and Preferences of Consumers. ...
The Consumer's Expectations. ...
The Number of Consumers in the Market.
What are the three factors affecting demand?
The demand for a product will be influenced by several factors:

Price. Usually viewed as the most important factor that affects demand.
...
Income levels. ...
Consumer tastes and preferences. ...
Competition. ...
Fashions.
What are the 4 factors of supply?
The four factors that can shift the supply curve include natural conditions, input prices, technology, and government.
What causes increase in supply?
If the cost of production is lower, the profits available at a given price will increase, and producers will produce more. With more produced at every price, the supply curve will shift to the right, meaning an increase in supply.
What causes supply changes?
A change in supply is an economic term that describes when the suppliers of a given good or service alter production or output. A change in supply can occur as a result of new technologies, such as more efficient or less expensive production processes, or a change in the number of competitors in the market.
Is supply and demand a good strategy?

When it comes to profit placement, supply and demand zones can be a great tool as well. Always place your profit target ahead of a zone so that you don't risk giving back all your profits when the open interest in that zone is filled.
How is demand created?
Demand creation is a process that fuels the revenue pipeline so the sales team can meet or exceed their quotas. In other words, it takes your big idea — the creative appeal of your brand — and turns it into sales. That sounds a lot like demand generation, which often gets confused with lead generation.
What are the two parts of demand?
Economists define demand as the quantity of a good or service that buyers are willing and able to buy at all possible prices during a certain time period.

Notice that there are two components to demand: willingness to purchase and ability to pay.

Can we control demand?

If you're willing to think and act strategically, you can easily manipulate the laws of supply and demand. It should be surprising to learn, however, that by manipulating the laws of supply and demand, you can make more profit in less time and with far fewer headaches

How do you control demand?

Here are five short-term actions to improve your demand variability management plans in this time of uncertainty:

Maintain transparent, proactive relationships with your suppliers. ...

Activate alternate sources of supply. ...

Reduce lead times. ...

Update inventory policy and planning. ...

Align supply and demand management.

What are the 8 types of demand?

There are 8 states of demand: negative demand, no demand, latent demand, falling demand, irregular demand, full demand, overfull demand and unwholesome demand.

What is Demand?

Types of Determinants of Demand. Every factor has a unique impact on demand. ...

Price of the Product. ...

The Income of the Consumers. ...

Number of Buyers in the Market. ...

Consumer's Expectations. ...

Tastes and Preferences of The Consumers. ...

Complement Goods. ...

Substitute Product.

What is theory of supply?

The law of supply is a fundamental principle of economic theory which states that, keeping other factors constant, an increase in price results in an increase in quantity supplied. In other words, there is a direct relationship between price and quantity: quantities respond in the same direction as price changes.

What are the types of supply?

There are five types of supply—market supply, short-term supply, long-term supply, joint supply, and composite supply.

Which comes first supply or demand?

Demand comes first and it's followed by the corresponding supplies. Supply and demand are both very important to economic activity. Supply is the total amount of a particular good or service available at a given time to consumers at a given price. Demand is a representation of a consumer's desire to purchase goods and services; it acts as a measurement of a consumer's willingness to purchase a specific good or service at a given price. These two economic forces influence each other; they are both important for the economy because they impact the prices of consumer goods and services within an economy and the quantities produced and consumed. Supply and demand are both keys to understanding the economy because they reflect the prices and quantities of consumer goods and services within an economy.

What are the relationship between demand and supply?

According to market economy theory, the relationship between supply and demand balances out at a point in the future; this point is called the equilibrium price.

Economists and companies analyze the relationship between supply and demand when making strategic product decisions. Both economists and companies analyze the relationship between supply and demand when making strategic product decisions. The assumption behind a market economy is that supply and demand are the best determinants for an economy's growth and health.

Consumer Behavior Influences Demand

One way that companies or economists might analyze this relationship is to create graphs that chart the equilibrium price of certain goods and services in order to determine product development and their production schedule. Consumer behavior dictates which products are produced and sold because consumers create the demand that companies attempt to meet. As a result, companies may study consumer behavior in an attempt to understand the current demand and predict future demand. It is vital that companies maintain the capacity to produce enough of a good or service that they can satisfy consumer demands.

Supply and demand are two sides of the same market coin. Generally, supply is how much of something is available or will be produced at a certain price. Demand is how much of something people want to purchase or consume at a certain price. One way to develop a more precise relationship between the two is to consider how the price of something affects its supply and its demand. Generally when the price of a good goes up, so does the supply, since firms are willing to create more when they can sell at higher prices. But when the price of a good goes up consumers will, at the same time, generally demand less. It is the interaction of supply and demand that determines how much will be produced and consumed and at what price, converging to a state known as equilibrium.

CHAPTER TWO

Human social job change demand and supply relationship

The relationship between social change and human behavior

Human Behavioral network job brings social economic benefits

Whether human social job change it depends on social job demand more or job supply more? What does human network job mean ? Why may human network job be popular? Why human network job behavior may influence economy ?

Nowadays internet is popular to use. We can apply internet to find data , search any new things, even earn money. Why does internet may become huma network job source. For example, e-publish may be one kind of new human network job. Any authors may apply internet channel to help them to sell electronic or paper books from e-publisher web store. They may apply facebook, you tub etc. any online channel to promote themselves new books to let new readers to know whether when they may buy themselves favourable new topic books to read from electronic publisher web store.

Thus, future electronic publisher industry may help any authors to build internet network platform to help them to sell and promote ot advertise their any one new electronic or paper book topic to let global any one reader to choose to buy their any new topic books from electronic publisher web store easily and conveniently. However, it implies that electronic network platform author may be one kind of future new human network job in our societies.

How electronic network platform author job may bring economy benefit in macro economy view? A person can have few friends, contacts and still be very influential if these few

friends and contacts are themselves highly influential, e.g. one author must not need to know any one reader in global society. When they like to choose any electronic books from electronic internet network platform. They may become the author's any one topic book buyer, when they feel the author's any one topic book is fun and attract they make decision to buth the strange author whose the topic book from electronic book publisher's platform web store conventiently in short time. Although, they are strangers, they do not know themselves , but the reader can understand what it way that made Google from writing platofrm to create new creative mind and typing network job method to replace traditional hand writing book method for global authors. It will be one kind of new human network writing job.

Hence, global any one reader can apply an innovative search engine , such as google.com to find whether whom author personal new topic books are value to read from internet.

Then, the electroniuc publisher's web store may be new book store platform sale network to help the author to sell many electronic or paper books from electronic network platform

in short time. So, internet may be future new network plaform to help global any one author to create network writing job absolutely. Furthermore, internet may be popular social media

to help any one author to build goold relationship between his/her readers. It is one kind of new network, human network job. New authors do not need to buy many paper books to prepare to put in any one book shop warehouse. Their every book can print on demand to reduce out of book stock in any one book shop. They may choose to sell either electronic books or paper books both from any one book publisher web store. So, electronic network platform may be one kind of good writing channel to help human authors to create income and it can also help authors to bring new creative mind and new topic fun content books to let readers to know and buy to read from electronic publisher network platform.

Why does human behavior may be one kind of new human network job to bring global economic advantages. ALthough, it may be free income or without inocme, but the person does the network behavior, his/her behavior may be bring advantages to influence many other people's health. For this case, when a worker in a coffee shop in an airport gets a vaccination aganinst the flu, it does not only helps him or her stay healthy, but also helps the many travellers who might otherwise have been inflected if that workers caught the flu. So, the externality , the result implies the vaccination of even a part of a community conveys benefits to the whole community. For example, governments pay special attention to the vaccinations of school children, teachers, health mothers, and the elderly, categories of people particularly susceptible not only to catching, but also to transmitting a disease.

It is not accidential that governments are heavily involved with vaccination . When there are externalities, free market, fail to persuade individual incentives with society's

their the worker's decision of whether to get a vaccine ends up attracting whether other people get sick. The workers might not fully take all these other people's potential suffering into account when making her or his vaccination decision.

As Stanford University does many suggestions, understand this and tries to help them make the right decisions and so providers free flu vaccines for its staff and students.

Small pockets of unvaccinated individuals can allow a disease to gain a spread more widely well-being. For example, parent weighing the costs and benefits of a vaccine for their child is not always thinking of the consequences of that vaccination to other people. THese are markets in which subsidizing or regulating behavior can make everyone better off. Because the reason for requiring that a child be vaccinated before enrolling in school is not just to protect that child, because each child's vaccination affects others via potential contagions.

On conclusion, it seems that many traditional paper book publish business begain to change to electronic book publish business. Due, to online technology existence, it influences many readers choose to buy electronic books to read. Hence, due to readers reading demand change which is from paper book reading habit to electonic book reading habit.Then,it explains that electornic book supply number depends on electronic book reader reading demand in economic view.

Robots take our jobs behavioral and economy influences

Robot job behavior brings economy influences

Whether robot labor needs are depended on employer labor demand more or robot labor number supply more? If one day robots can replace human to do simple, even complex jobs. They will bring what influences to our global societial economy.The popular economic refrain declares that the
global middle class is dying and robots will soon take our jobs, e.g. shopping center customer service jobs, library service jobs, cinema ticket sale jobs, restaurant kitchen cooker jobs,
even, bus drivers, taxi drivers etc. public transport driving jobs, accountant, doctors etc. professional jobs. Whether it is beautiful or petty matter if our future societies have many human jobs can be replaced to do from robots. Businessman must may reduce to employ employees and reduce to pay salary or wage, when robots can be replaced to do their employees tasks. But, societies must bring unemployement rate rises , due to societies will have many people loss jobs when their employers choose to buy robots to serve their clients or do any office tasks or customer service or cleaning etc. tasks.

In micro economy view, employers may save money in long term, but in macro economy view, it will cause unemployment ratio rises , even crime rate rises when there are many people lose
jobs in societies. These models of doom, though, fail to account for the hundreds of businesses riding the waves of change in their industries when robots may be invented to replace human to do many simple , even complex tasks in our future societies.

WE may image that one small factory needs to manufacture fishes canes to sell to supermarket, the small , cheaper stuff and higher margin parts of the fishes manufacture industry. Before, this factory needs to employe many human factory workers need to help every fresh customer makeing the perfect fishing gear, designed for performance, durability, and cost in order to achieve to manufacture every fish cane in whole fished processing manufacturing stages. Every worker needs to spend about 15 to twenty minutes to finish every fish cane , till to delivery to any supermarket to sell. If this fish canes manufacturing factory can apply manufacturing robots to help them to finish any one working tasks , every robot can only spend five minutes to finish whole fresh fish cane manufacturing process. Thus, every robot can
help this factory save 10 to 15 minutes time to finsh every fish cane

manufacturing process. IN fact, time is money, because when every robot can help this factory to reduce 10 to 15 minutes time to compare human worker. Then, this factory can finish about 20 fish canes in one hour if it can use robot to help it to manufacture fish canes. Otherwise, if this factory still use human workers to help it to manufacture fish canes, then it can finsh about 3 to 4 fish canes in one hour. SO, the manufacturing efficiency ensures that robots must help this fish manufacturing factory to raise fish canes number more than human workers. So, in robotic behavioral economy view, manufacturing robots must help this fish canes manufacturing factory to raise fish canes manufacturing number and deliver increasing number to supermarkets to prepare to sell every day. Robots can help this fish canes manufacturing factory bring manufacturing time saving, rising manufacturing efficiency, improving performance and reducing wages expenditure long time advantages in micro economy view. However, manufacturing robots can also bring disadvanages to society, e.g. increasing unemployment ratio, increasing crime rate,
this factory workers will lose jobs and income, they need earn social welfare from government and increasing government finance pressure in short time, even long time in macro economic view.

Stanford University graduate program in economics, Scott lecturer explained that "in demand and supply economic theory for robots supply and demand case, robots supply number increasing may influence human workers demand number decrease. It sometimes calls " the efficient frontier".
No specific human beings were mentioned in any of economics classes. As robots supply and demand in market case, They (robots) may be purely theoretical " agents" who reached to the most reasonable sale prices in order to persuade any one businessman buyer to make manufacturing robot buying decision whether robots can help him / her to bring how much saving time , saving money, saving cost, improving performance, efficiency economic benefit before he/she plans to reduce workers number when he/ she decides to apply robots to replace human workers in his/her factory or office or any service department, e.g. cinema ticket sale service, shopping center customer service, shopping center cleaning , supermarket customer service etc. service or sale tasks. When robots can replace human to do any one of these tasks in any organizations. So, robots may be human worker agents who reached to prices the way robots would react to a software command. There was nothing that explained why some people thrived

and others did n't or why truly brilliant, hardworking people could fail when much lazier folks succeeded." Having been admitted to the Stanford University graduate program in economics, Scott lecturer hoped to get his answers there.

How robots influence our future social changing? Using the right technology can be a boon to your business in this economy. For internet example, it is easier than ever to find well-matched customers all around the world, to stay in contact with them, and to more quickly design the products they want. If you focus solely on being cutting -edge, though you risk letting the technology

take over what should be very robust relationships with your customers , employees, and colleagues. IN nowaddays society, technoligical advances and cutomation, personal

relationships in business are more crucial than ever. I mean that robots can not replace human to serve clients to let them to feel more comfortable and passion more easily. For shoe shop case example, if the shoe shop apply one robot to serve its clients to replace human shoe salesperson to serve its shoe customers. Robots ensure that they can not persuade every shoe potential buyer to make shoe buying decision more easily when robots need to contact every shoe potential buyer. The reason is simple, because robots can not touch any one shoe buyer individual emotion very easier.

If the shoe buyer needs the robots to help him/her to choose any right shoe styles when he/she can not feel himself / herself can make the most right shoe style choice decision. The robots can not replace human shoe salesperson to make shoe style choice judgement more easily. They must need longer time to analyze whether which shoe style may be the most suitable to the shoe buyer. Otherwise, human shoe salesperson may attempt to make the most right shoe style choice decision to help any one shoe buyer to chooce the most right style shoe because he/she owns shoe style sale experience, shoe style knowledge, the most important reason is that they can feel every shoe customer individual emotion to touch whether he/she will feel comfortable or happy when they attempt to help every shoe customer to seek the most right shoe style in every shoe customer whole shoe searching processing. Othwerwise, serving robots are only one machine, they can not touch or feel every shoe customer individual emotion whether he/she feel comfortable or unhappy or happy when they need to contact them in whole shoe searching processing. Hence, I believe that some tasks robots can

not repalce human staff to do very easily. Otherwise, robots may bring disadvanatges to let any one businessman to loss his/her customers, due to robots can not touch every customer
emotion to compare human staff in service tasks more easily. Robots serving customer behaviors may cause money lose and customers number lose to the shop in micro economic view.

On conclusion, in demand and supply economic theory for robots supply and demand case, robots supply number increasing may influence human workers demand number decrease. So, it seems that robots number supply will be depended on global robots supply number more than robots demand number because when human began to accept robots to replace human to do general simple jobs in global labor market. Then, it means that global robots labor number must need to be increased in order to satisfy global businessmen workers number need. If any kinds of robot workers manufacture number is not enough to be supplied to let global future businessmen to buy, then robot supply will be shortage and they can not provide to satisfy global businessmen robots labour purchase need. So, future robot number will be depended on supply more than demand.

CHAPTER THREE

Human intellectual demand and supply behavior relationship

Intellectual human economic behaviors

What does intellectual human economic behaviors mean ? Human foolish behavior is depended on social enjoyment need more or material social supply more? I believe that when we choose or decide to do intellectual behaviors, then our societies will be influenced to bring economic growth in consequence.I shall attempt to indicate pollution case to explain how and why eithet our intellectual or foolish behaviors may bring economic growth or recession in consequence as below:

On one hand, for air pollution social case aspect example, if we only consider to buy cars to drive for working aim or holiday leisure aim. Then, our societies air will be polluted. Our health will be influenced to bad. Our car driving behaviors may cause global environment air pollution serously. In long tiem, global air pollution will bring our bodies health to be bad. Although, ourselves car driving behaviors may bring our driving travelling leisure enjoyment and comfortable feeling in short time, also we so not need to pay public transport fare often, but we need to compensate ourselves health economic intangible loss due to air pollution , when cars number increases, dirty air will cause ouselves health to become bad.

In the result, we will need to pay more medical expenditure when we are old age, due to ourselves bodies will become bad, due to we breathe global dirty air every day, due to ourselves cars pollute air in long time, e.g. 10 to 20 years, even 30 more without limited air pollution environment. So, driving cars behavior may be one kind of human foolish behavior and our foolish behavior may bring ourselves future long time medical expenditure absolutely.

One the other hand, water pollution social aspect, if we often keep much rubblish to pollute sea, oil exploration porcessing pollute ocean , ships gas pollute ocaen, then fishes will eat polluted food and drive dirty water, due to global ocean is polluted.

In fact, because human only to conside how to buy boats to carry on leisure enjoyment activities, or catch cruises to travel on the sea. Also, oil manufacturers only consider researching anywhere to find new oil exploration places to manufacture oil product, when their oil exploration processes pollute ocarn . Consequently, global fishes drink polluted warer or eat polluted food. They will have poison. SO, human will have high chance to eat poison polluted fishes, due to fishes are poison or are polluted. So, human is doing foolish activities, we only hope to find oil exploration places to pollute ocean or we only spend money to buy ticket to catch ships to travel anywhere in global ocean. All of these human foolish behaviors will bring pollution to global ocean. On consequently, we will need to compensate to eat polluted or dirty or poision fishes, ourselves bodies health will be bad. In long time, we need have high chance to pay medical expenditure when we are old. So, pollution case may be one good example to explain how and why human foolish behavior may influence ourselves future need to compensate serious medical loss.

All of these human foolish behavior will bring pollution to global ocean. On consequently, we will need to compensate to eat polluted or dirty or poison fished , ourselves bodies health will be bad. In long time, we will have high chance to pay medical expenditure, when we are old. So, pollution case may be one good example to explain how and why human ourselves intellectual or foolish behaviors may influence future long time economic loss or economic growth or recession in micro and micro economic view.

On another water pollution aspect hand, if we often keep rubbish to sea, oil exploration processing pollutes ocean and ships' gas pollute ocean, then fishes will eat polluted food and drink dirty water, due to fishes will eat polluted food and drink dirty sea water because the global ocean is polluted seriously.

In fact, because human only consider how to buy boats to carry on any leisure water activities, or catches cruises to travel on the sea. Also, oil manufacturers only consider any where to find oil exploratin places to manufacture oil products from ocean, when their pol exploration processes can plooute ocean. Consequently, global fishes drink polluted water or eat direty food. They will have poison. So, human will have high chance to eat poison fishes.

Otherwise, such as pollutin case, it can infuence inflation or deflation. Consequently, the reason indicates supply and demand theory. If air pollution is serious, then we will consider health issue, global cars demand number may be influenced to reduce, when global cars number demand will reduce, global car prices and supply number will need to change to fall down in order to attract or persuade global car consumers choose to make car purchase decision.

Hence, global car manufacture number and car price will be influenced to reduce, due to global air pollution issue. Consequently, deflation will occur because when the country citizen usually does not spend much extra saving money to buy car expensive goods. Money value will be low. Otherwise, if global cair pollution is not serious, human considers to buy cars to enjoy driving leisure lives. So, global car demand is influenced to increase , also global car price will also influenced to increase.

Consequently, gobal human will choose to buy cars to drive. Due to we accept to spend extra saving to buy expensive car goods. Car sale price and supply may be influenced to rise up. Money value is influenced to reduce. Inflation may be influenced, due to global car consumers number increases, we would not have extra money to spend easily. Car expensive goods expenditure influences our spending habit to avoid to make car purchase decision more easily. So, human intellectual or foolish activities may bring inflation or deflation consequency in possible indirectly in macro economic view.

On conclusion, above pollution case explain that how and why human intellectual or foolish economic behaviors may bring inflation or deflation consequency as wll as economic growth or recession consequency as well as any goods demand and supply increasing or decreasing consequency. It implies that human behavior may have indirect relationship to influence any goods demand and supply number to either increase or decrease result as well as any goods price will be influenced to increase or decrease in micro and macro economic view. Hence, Human foolish behavior is depended on social enjoyment need more or material social supply more because human needs to raise enjoyment feel , so we will choose to do foolish behavior, e.g. air pollution, when many people choose to buy cars to drive to replace catch public transport. So, such as car market, it depends on car demand number more than car supply number absolutely in demand and supply view.

The relationship between social change and human behavior

Why does economic changes may influence human individual behavioral change? I shall attempt to indicate shopping behavior and staying at home behavior to explain their case and effect relationsip as below:

Human behavior can be influenced by economic change or economic change can be influenced by human behavior? Why does recession may influence consumers reduce shopping desire? In social recession suitation, it is possible that many people lose jobs suddenly, due to businessmen lose many customers. They need to make decision to reduce employees number in order to continue to keep businesses. Consequently, many firms (organizations) their employees may lose jobs. When they have much time, due to lose jobs, they will feel to avoid to spend too much time and money to go to shopping often. Many losing jobs people, they will often stay at homes. So, they will reduce time to go to shopping, then non essential products won't their preferable choice purchase products. Hence, recession will change many losing jobs people their shopping or consumption desires to avoid to buy non essential products often . Usually when economic boom, many people have jobs to do because consumers number must increase when many people have jobs to do. Then, many people can accept to spend money to buy non essential products often. Many people feel spend time to go to shopping can satisfy their purchase of any kinds of new products useful psychology or desire. So, recession is one good example to explain it can influence many people do not like often to leave homes to go to shopping easily. Many people like to stay at homes, becaue they feel worry about spending too much shopping time when they leave homes. Their staying home time is one good negative shopping behavior example. So, economic change may influence human individual behavior changes , they have direct cause and efect relationsip in behavioral economic view.

May human behavior influence economic change? Is it possible that human behavior may bring the country social economic change in macro economic or micro behavioral economic view ? I shall indicate publishing industry example. Do you feel that if there are many students feel learning is very important when they read many books or many of students feel interesting to read or they have reading new books in habit, then it is possible that the country will have many students like to spend time to go to any book shops to choose the books, they feel that they can help they learn new knowledge.

Then the country will increase students number, they often spend time to visit any one book shop every week. Their visiting book shops behavior which may become their habits. So, the country will increase students number, they often spend time to visit book shops. Also, it implies that visiting book shops behaviors may be their behavioral habits.

So, when the country has many students often spend time to visit book shops , their visiting book shops behaviors may help any one book shop to raise books sale chance. So, the country's student individual often visiting book shop behaviors, their habitual visiting book shops behaviors must may assist help any one book shop to increase books sale number absolutely.

Consequently, any one book shop , its books sale bumber must be influenced to increase to increase because the country will have many students like or feel need visit book shops habit in order to choose any suitable books to buy to read at home in order to raise themselves learning effort. When the country has many bok shops often have many students visit their book shops, then their books sale number may be influenced to increase. It explain why student individual visiting book shop behavior may help any one book shop sale number increases also. So, visiting shops products sale number is depended on online products supply number, if online products supply number increases, then it may cause many customers choose to buy the kind of products from online webstore. So, any shop products sale number will depend on onlint products supply number in supply and demand view.

CHAPTER FOUR

Technology or human behavior whether may influence economic growth or recession

Human Behavioral network job brings social economic benefits

What does human network job mean ? Why may human network job be popular? Why human network job behavior may influence economy ? Nowadays internet is popular to use. We can apply internet to find data , search any new things, even earn money. Why does internet

may become huma network job source. For example, e-publish may be one kind of new human network job. Any authors may apply internet

channel to help them to sell electronic or paper books from e-publisher web store. They may apply facebook, you tub etc. any online

channel to promote themselves new books to let new readers to know whether when they may buy themselves favourable new topic books to read from electronic publisher web store.

Thus, future electronic publisher industry may help any authors to build internet network platform to help them to sell and promote

ot advertise their any one new electronic or paper book topic to let global any one reader to choose to buy their any new topic books from electronic publisher web store easily and conveniently. However, it implies that electronic network platform author may be one kind of future new human network job in our societies.

How electronic network platform author job may bring economy benefit in macro economy view? A person can have few friends, contacts and still be very influential if these few

friends and contacts are themselves highly influential, e.g. one author must not need to know any one reader in global society. When they like to choose any electronic books from electronic internet network platform. They may become the author's any one topic book buyer, when they feel the author's any one topic book is fun and attract they make decision to buth the strange author whose the topic book from electronic book publisher's platform web store conventiently in short time. Although, they are strangers, they do not know themselves , but the reader can understand what it way that made Google from writing platofrm to create new creative mind and typing network job method to replace traditional hand writing book method for global authors. It will be one kind of new human network writing job.

Hence, global any one reader can apply an innovative search engine , such as google.com to find whether whom author personal new topic books are value to read from internet.

Then, the electroniuc publisher's web store may be new book store platform sale network to help the author to sell many electronic or paper books from electronic network platform

in short time. So, internet may be future new network plaform to help global any one author to create network writing job absolutely. Furthermore, internet may be popular social media

to help any one author to build goold relationship between his/her readers. It is one kind of new network, human network job. New authors do not need to buy many paper books to prepare to put in any one book shop warehouse. Their every book can print on demand to reduce out of book stock in any one book shop. They may choose to sell either electronic books or paper books both from any one book publisher web store. So, electronic network platform may be one kind of good writing channel to help human authors to create income and it can also help authors to bring new creative mind and new topic fun content books to let readers to know and buy to read from electronic publisher network platform.

Why does human behavior may be one kind of new human network job to bring global economic advantages. ALthough, it may be free income or without inocme, but the person does the network behavior, his/her behavior may be bring advantages to influence many other people's health. For this case, when a worker in a coffee shop in an airport gets a vaccination aganinst the flu, it does not only helps him or her stay healthy, but also helps the many travellers who might otherwise have been inflected if that workers caught the flu. So, the externality , the result implies the vaccination of even a part of a community conveys benefits to the whole community. For example, governments pay special attention to the vaccinations of school children, teachers, health mothers, and the elderly, categories of people particularly susceptible not only to catching, but also to transmitting a disease.

It is not accidental that governments are heavily involved with vaccination . When there are externalities, free market, fail to persuade individual incentives with society's

their the worker's decision of whether to get a vaccine ends up attracting whether other people get sick. The workers might not fully take all these other people's potential suffering into account when making her or his vaccination decision.

As Stanford University does many suggestions, understand this and tries to help them make the right decisions and so providers free flu vaccines for its staff and students.

Small pockets of unvaccinated individuals can allow a disease to gain a spread more widely well-being. For example, parent weighing the costs and benefits of a vaccine for their child is not always thinking of the consequences of that vaccination to other people. THese are markets in which subsidizing or regulating behavior can make everyone better off. Because the reason for requiring that a child be vaccinated before enrolling in school is not just to protect that child, because each child's vaccination affects others via potential contagions.

Robots take our jobs behavioral and economy influences

Robot job behavior brings economy influences

If one day robots can replace human to do simple, even complex jobs. They will bring what influences to our global societial economy.The popular economic refrain declares that the

global middle class is dying and robots will soon take our jobs, e.g. shopping center customer service jobs, library service jobs, cinema ticket sale jobs, restaurant kitchen cooker jobs,

even, bus drivers, taxi drivers etc. public transport driving jobs, accountant, doctors etc. professional jobs. Whether it is beautiful or petty matter if our future societies have many human jobs can be replaced to do from robots.

Businessman must may reduce to employ employees and reduce to pay salary or wage, when robots can be replaced to do their employees tasks. But, societies must bring unemployement rate rises , due to societies will have many people loss jobs when their employers choose to buy robots to serve their clients or do any office tasks or customer service or cleaning etc. tasks.

In micro economy view, employers may save money in long term, but in macro economy view, it will cause unemployment ratio rises , even crime rate rises when there are many people lose
jobs in societies. These models of doom, though, fail to account for the hundreds of businesses riding the waves of change in their industries when robots may be invented to replace human to do many simple , even complex tasks in our future societies.

WE may image that one small factory needs to manufacture fishes canes to sell to supermarket, the small , cheaper stuff and higher margin parts of the fishes manufacture industry. Before, this factory needs to employe many human factory workers need to help every fresh customer makeing the perfect fishing gear, designed for performance, durability, and cost in order to achieve to manufacture every fish cane in whole fished processing manufacturing stages. Every worker needs to spend about 15 to twenty minutes to finish every fish cane , till to delivery to any supermarket to sell. If this fish canes manufacturing factory can apply manufacturing robots to help them to finish any one working tasks , every robot can only spend five minutes to finish whole fresh fish cane manufacturing process. Thus, every robot can
help this factory save 10 to 15 minutes time to finsh every fish cane manufacturing process. IN fact, time is money, because when every robot can help this factory to reduce 10 to 15 minutes time to compare human worker. Then, this factory can finish about 20 fish canes in one hour if it can use robot to help it to manufacture fish canes. Otherwise, if this factory still use human workers to help it to manufacture fish canes, then it can finsh about 3 to 4 fish canes in one hour. SO, the manufacturing efficiency ensures that robots must help this fish manufacturing factory to raise fish canes number more than human workers. So, in robotic behavioral economy view, manufacturing robots must help this fish canes manufacturing factory to raise fish canes manufacturing number and deliver increasing number to supermarkets to prepare to sell every day. Robots can help this fish canes manufacturing factory bring manufacturing time saving,

rising manufacturing efficiency, improving performance and reducing wages expenditure long time advantages in micro economy view. However, manufacturing robots can also bring disadvanages to society, e.g. increasing unemployment ratio, increasing crime rate,
this factory workers will lose jobs and income, they need earn social welfare from government and increasing government finance pressure in short time, even long time in macro economic view.

Stanford University graduate program in economics, Scott lecturer explained that "in demand and supply economic theory for robots supply and demand case, robots supply number increasing may influence human workers demand number decrease. It sometimes calls " the efficient frontier".

No specific human beings were mentioned in any of economics classes. As robots supply and demand in market case, They (robots) may be purely theoretical " agents" who reached to the most reasonable sale prices in order to persuade any one businessman buyer to make manufacturing robot buying decision whether robots can help him / her to bring how much saving time , saving money, saving cost, improving performance, efficiency economic benefit before he/she plans to reduce workers number when he/ she decides to apply robots to replace human workers in his/her factory or office or any service department, e.g. cinema ticket sale service, shopping center customer service, shopping center cleaning , supermarket customer service etc. service or sale tasks. When robots can replace human to do any one of these tasks in any organizations. So, robots may be human worker agents who reached to prices the way robots would react to a software
command. There was nothing that explained why some people thrived and others did n't or why truly brilliant, hardworking people could fail when much lazier folks succeeded." Having been admitted to the Stanford University graduate program in economics, Scott lecturer hoped to get his answers there.

How robots influence our future social changing? Using the right technology can be a boon to your business in this economy. For internet example, it is easier than ever to find well-matched customers all around the world, to stay in contact with them, and to more quickly design the products they want. If you focus solely on being cutting -edge, though you risk letting the technology
take over what should be very robust relationships with your customers , employees, and colleagues. IN nowaddays society, technoligical advances

and cutomation, personal

relationships in business are more crucial than ever. I mean that robots can not replace human to serve clients to let them to feel more comfortable and passion more easily. For shoe shop case example, if the shoe shop apply one robot to serve its clients to replace human shoe salesperson to serve its shoe customers. Robots ensure that they can not persuade every shoe potential buyer to make shoe buying decision more easily when robots need to contact every shoe potential buyer. The reason is simple, because robots can not touch any one shoe buyer individual emotion very easier.

If the shoe buyer needs the robots to help him/her to choose any right shoe styles when he/she can not feel himself / herself can make the most right shoe style choice decision. The robots can not replace human shoe salesperson to make shoe style choice judgement more easily. They must need longer time to analyze whether which shoe style may be the most suitable to the shoe buyer. Otherwise, human shoe salesperson may attempt to make the most right shoe style choice decision to help any one shoe buyer to chooce the most right style shoe because he/she owns shoe style sale experience, shoe style knowledge, the most important reason is that they can feel every shoe customer individual emotion to touch whether he/she will feel comfortable or happy when they attempt to help every shoe customer to seek the most right shoe style in every shoe customer whole shoe searching processing. Othwerwise, serving robots are only one machine, they can not touch or feel every shoe customer individual emotion whether he/she feel comfortable or unhappy or happy when they need to contact them in whole shoe searching processing. Hence, I believe that some tasks robots can

not repalce human staff to do very easily. Otherwise, robots may bring disadvanatges to let any one businessman to loss his/her customers, due to robots can not touch every customer

emotion to compare human staff in service tasks more easily. Robots serving customer behaviors may cause money lose and customers number lose to the shop in micro economic view.

Intellectual human economic behaviors

What does intellectual human economic behaviors mean ? I believe that when we choose or decide to do intellectual behaviors, then our societies will be influenced to bring economic growth in consequence.I shall attempt to indicate pollution case to explain how and why eithet our intellectual or foolish behaviors may bring economic growth or recession in consequence as below:

On one hand, for air pollution social case aspect example, if we only consider to buy cars to drive for working aimr or holiday leisure aim. Then, our societies air will be polluted. Our health will be influenced to bad. Our car driving behaviors may cause global environment air pollution serously. In long tiem, global air pollution will bring our bodies health to be bad. Although, ourselves car driving behaviors may bring our driving travelling leisure enjoyment and comfortable feeling in short time, also we so not need to pay public transport fare often, but we need to compensate ourselves health economic intangible loss due to air pollution , when cars number increases, dirty air will cause ouselves health to become bad.

In the result, we will need to pay more medical expenditure when we are old age, due to ourselves bodies will become bad, due to we breathe global dirty air every day, due to ourselves cars pollute air in long time, e.g. 10 to 20 years, even 30 more without limited air pollution environment. So, driving cars behavior may be one kind of human foolish behavior and our foolish behavior may bring ourselves future long time medical expenditure absolutely.

One the other hand, water pollution social aspect, if we often keep much rubblish to pollute sea, oil exploration porcessing pollute ocean , ships gas pollute ocaen, then fishes will eat polluted food and drive dirty water, due to global ocean is polluted.

In fact, because human only to conside how to buy boats to carry on leisure enjoyment activities, or catch cruises to travel on the sea. Also, oil manufacturers only consider researching anywhere to find new oil exploration places to manufacture oil product, when their oil exploration processes pollute ocarn . Consequently, global fishes drink polluted warer or eat polluted food. They will have poison. SO, human will have high chance to eat poison polluted fishes, due to fishes are poison or are polluted. So, human is doing foolish activities, we only hope to find oil exploration places to pollute ocean or we only spend money to buy ticket to catch ships to travel anywhere in global ocean. All of these human foolish behaviors will bring pollution to global ocean. On consequently, we will need to compensate to eat polluted or dirty or poision fishes, ourselves bodies health will be bad. In long time, we need have high chance to pay medical expenditure when we are old. So, pollution case may be one good example to explain how and why human foolish behavior may influence ourselves future need to compensate serious medical loss.

All of these human foolish behavior will bring pollution to global ocean. On consequently, we will need to compensate to eat polluted or dirty or poison fished , ourselves bodies health will be bad. In long time, we will have high chance to pay medical expenditure, when we are old. So, pollution case may be one good example to explain how and why human ourselves intellectual or foolish behaviors may influence future long time economic loss or economic growth or recession in micro and micro economic view.

On another water pollution aspect hand, if we often keep rubbish to sea, oil exploration processing pollutes ocean and ships' gas pollute ocean, then fishes will eat polluted food and drink dirty water, due to fishes will eat polluted food and drink dirty sea water because the global ocean is polluted seriously.

In fact, because human only consider how to buy boats to carry on any leisure water activities, or catches cruises to travel on the sea. Also, oil manufacturers only consider any where to find oil exploratin places to manufacture oil products from ocean, when their pol exploration processes can plooute ocean. Consequently, global fishes drink polluted water or eat direty food. They will have poison. So, human will have high chance to eat poison fishes.

Otherwise, such as pollutin case, it can infuence inflation or deflation. Consequently, the reason indicates supply and demand theory. If air pollution is serious, then we will consider health issue, global cars demand number may be influenced to reduce, when global cars number demand will reduce, global car prices and supply number will need to change to fall down in order to attract or persuade global car consumers choose to make car purchase decision.

Hence, global car manufacture number and car price will be influenced to reduce, due to global air pollution issue. Consequently, deflation will occur because when the country citizen usually does not spend much extra saving money to buy car expensive goods. Money value will be low. Otherwise, if global cair pollution is not serious, human considers to buy cars to enjoy driving leisure lives. So, global car demand is influenced to increase , also global car price will also influenced to increase.

Consequently, gobal human will choose to buy cars to drive. Due to we accept to spend extra saving to buy expensive car goods. Car sale price and supply may be influenced to rise up. Money value is influenced to reduce. Inflation may be influenced, due to global car consumers number increases, we would not have extra money to spend easily. Car expensive goods expenditure influences our spending habit to avoid to make car purchase decision more easily. So, human intellectual or foolish activities may bring inflation or deflation consequency in possible indirectly in macro economic view.

On conclusion, above pollution case explain that how and why human intellectual or foolish economic behaviors may bring inflation or deflation consequency as wll as economic growth or recession consequency as well as any goods demand and supply increasing or decreasing consequency. It implies that human behavior may have indirect relationship to influence any goods demand and supply number to either increase or decrease result as well as any goods price will be influenced to increase or decrease in micro and macro economic view.

The relationship between social change and human behavior

Why does economic changes may influence human individual behavioral change? I shall attempt to indicate shopping behavior and staying at home behavior to explain their case and effect relationsip as below:

Human behavior can be influenced by economic change or economic change can be influenced by human behavior? Why does recession may influence consumers reduce shopping desire? In social recession suitation, it is possible that many people lose jobs suddenly, due to businessmen lose many customers. They need to make decision to reduce employees number in order to continue to keep businesses. Consequently, many firms (organizations) their employees may lose jobs. When they have much time, due to lose jobs, they will feel to avoid to spend too much time and money to go to shopping often. Many losing jobs people, they will often stay at homes. So, they will reduce time to go to shopping, then non essential products won't their preferable choice purchase products. Hence, recession will change many losing jobs people their shopping or consumption desires to avoid to buy non essential products often . Usually when economic boom, many people have jobs to do because consumers number must increase when many people have jobs to do. Then, many people can accept to spend money to buy non essential products often. Many people feel spend time to go to shopping can satisfy their purchase of any kinds of new products useful psychology or desire. So, recession is one good example to explain it can influence many people do not like often to leave homes to go to shopping easily. Many people like to stay at homes, becaue they feel worry about spending too much shopping time when they leave homes. Their staying home time is one good negative shopping behavior example. So, economic change may influence human individual behavior changes , they have direct cause and efect relationship in behavioral economic view.

May human behavior influence economic change? Is it possible that human behavior may bring the country social economic change in macro economic or micro behavioral economic view ? I shall indicate publishing industry example. Do you feel that if there are many students feel learning is very important when they read many books or many of students feel interesting to read or they have reading new books in habit, then it is possible that the country will have many students like to spend time to go to any book shops to choose the books, they feel that they can help they learn new knowledge. Then the country will increase students number, they often spend time to visit any one book shop every week. Their visiting book shops behavior which may become their habits. So, the country will increase students number, they often spend time to visit book shops. Also, it implies that visiting book shops behaviors may be their behavioral habits.

So, when the country has many students often spend time to visit book shops , their visiting book shops behaviors may help any one book shop to raise books sale chance. So, the country's student individual often visiting book shop behaviors, their habitual visiting book shops behaviors must may assist help any one book shop to increase books sale number absolutely.

Consequently, any one book shop , its books sale bumber must be influenced to increase to increase because the country will have many students like or feel need visit book shops habit in order to choose any suitable books to buy to read at home in order to raise themselves learning effort. When the country has many bok shops often have many students visit their book shops, then their books sale number may be influenced to increase. It explain why student individual visiting book shop behavior may help any one book shop sale number increases also.

How human productive behavior may influence economic development

May any country which citizen behavior assist themselves country development? It is one cause and effect economic question. I mean that if the country itself citicen can not concentrate mind or energy to choose to do one kind of industry in order to let themselves country can bring the most benefit, then whether the counry itself economy can bring the most serious economic benefit. I shall attempt to indicate these countries themselves indistry choice to explain whether these countries themselves citizen productive behavior may help themselves countries to achieve the largest economic benefits. I shall indicate as below:

New Zealand farmer individual wine productive behavior

For New Zealand country example, this country concerns itself effort is foucs on farming agricultural aspect. So, this country has many farmers concentrate on farming agricultural aspect. May New Zealanders choose to spend time to produce different kinds of wines, e.g. wine or red grape wine is for the people are eating meat, or they are eating dinner.

When these New Zealanders their behaviors choose to do farming or agriculture to grow and produce different kinds of taste of white or red grape wine drinking products job. Themselves grape agriculture behavior will influence these New Zealanders themselves, they can learn how to improve different kinds of grape wine drinking products in order to achieve every kinds of white or read grape wines taste improving aim during their white or red grape producing process.

Why can New Zealander every individual white or read grape wine producers improve their white or read grape wine taste more easily? In behavioral economic view, it can explain that why any one New Zealander white or read grape wine producer can be encouraged or excited or persuaded to concentrate nervous and energy and effort to learn how to improve their white or red grape wine products easily.

In fact, New Zealand is one agricultural food export country. It has good natural environment resource , e.g. land, seed to provide any one farmer to produce themselves any kinds of agricultrual food products, e.g. fruit, or wine food products. Because New Zealanders know themselves country has enough natural resource . So, in common, many New Zealanders choose to attempt to do farming agricultural jobs in order to export themselves any kinds of fruit or meat or wine products to overseas or sell to domestic in order to earn profit.

So, when these New Zealand farmers number has been increasing every year. This country farmers will feel themsleves competition between this New Zealand farmers themselves are serious due to they may feel New Zealanders choose to do agriculture businesses in order to export themselves different kinds of farming food to overseas or sell to local to earn profit.

Hence, when many New Zealand farmers feel that farmers number has been increasing every year. They will feel themselves competition is serious. They must need to spend much time and nervous and effort to research what method is the best how to produce the best taste of white or red grape wine products in order to let local or overseas wine buyers to choose to buy his/her producing white or read grpae products to drink.

Hence, in competition psychological view, may influence many New Zealand white or reaad wine producers had been beginning to change their learning behavior on researching what method is the best in order to produce the best quality of taste red or white wine products to sell in order to attract overseas or local white or read grape wine drinkers to choose to buy his/her wine products. Their behavior will focus on learning how to raising or improving white or read grape wine taste method more than only focus on producing a large number white or red grape wine products. They believe wine quality is more important to compare wine producing number. So, New Zealand wine producers themselves wine producers behaviors have been changing on concentrating on researching wine quality method aspect more then wine producing number aspect in behavioral economic view.

America high technological productive behavior

For America example, US is one high technological country, it owns many high technological knowledge talent inventors, e.g. computer science inventors. Hence, US must attract many diferent countries owning high technological computer inventors choose to go to US to develop their computer science profession career. Also, it seems that when many computer science inventors or professions choose to go to US to develop themselves computer science new career. In behavioral economic view, due to their leaving themselves countries choice, which may bring influence themselve country job behaviors need to be changed. They must need to adapt US new live. Because they will forgive their past computer science job. These computer science professionals need to spend time to adapt US new lives. They " past computer science job behaviors" will need to be changed to their new US any computer employer's new computer science job model.

Because their traditional computer science jobs needed to be forgot in their themselves countries. They will feel their old computer science job knowledge and behavior needed to change in order to let their US any one new of computer company employer feels satisfactory to accept their new working behavior in any one US computer organization.

So, on the other hand, many US computer company employer will feel that they must need time to accept any one new overseas computer science professions their working behaviors, their working attitude daily, because these foreign comouter science professional, their past computer working behaviors and working attitude must be different to US domestic computer science professions.

In behavioral economic view, these overseas computer science professions, their working behaviors and attitude must be needed to change in order to adapt any one US new computer company itself domestic or local computer science professional stafs themselves daily working behaviors and attitude because these overseas and local computer science professionals must need to team work together.

In behavioral economic view, it is only one way that foreign computer science professionals must need to change themselves past country traditiona daily working behaviors and attitude in order to cooperate with these US local computer science professionals in teams more easily.

Consequently, if these foreign compute science professionals can change their past working behaviors and attitude to let any one US local computer science professional feels to cooperate with them easily in short time. Then, the US computer company itself whole computer professional teams themselves efficiencies will be influenced to raised or improved by the changing past working attitude and working behaviors of these foreign computer science professionals. So, in behavioral economic view, only if US any one computer company hopes itself computer teams themselves efficiency can be raised or improved when it decides to employ foreign computer science professionals and US domestic computer science professionals. They need to work in teams together. They must need to let these foreign computer science professionals to know how to change their working behaviors and attitude to let their domestic computer science professionals feel easy to work together. Then, the US computer company itself whole team efficiency must be rasied or improved easily in short time.

● China share market investing behavior

For China share market example, economic development depends on financial market. Because if many Chinese have interest to invest to carry on shares buying and selling activities in orde to learn how to earn shares interest and share profit when the China shareholder can make decision to sell himself/herself shares in the the high price, then he/she can earn money when he/she can sell the China company's shares in the high sale share price position.

If China has many Chinese like to spend time to carry on investing shares activities. Themselves shares buying and selling behaviors will influence China has many companies can increase fund from many Chinese shareholders in order to have enough money to expand or develop themselves businesses in China in long term.

Consequently, when China can have many Chinese like to attempt to carry on buying and selling shares investing behaviors in China share market. Themselves buying and selling shares behaviors can help many Chinese companies have effort to increase enough money or capital in order to continue to do their businesses in long term absolutely. So, it explains why when many Chinese become shareholders , they can assist China will have many companies continue to develop their businesses if many Chinese like to carry on shares buying and selling investing behaviors in long time in China financial investment market nowadays in behavioral economic view.

Why has any individual country have many people invest share behavior which can influence the country's macro consumption desire?

I shall apply shares market buying and selling investment behavior to explaiin why shares investment behavior which may impact the country's overal consumption desire as below:

In behavioral economic view, I assume that when the coutry has many people have interest to attempt to carry on shares buying and selling investment behavior, then their frequent shares buying and selling behaviors which may bring negactive consumption desire or shopping desire of these shares investors their consumer behavior.

The reason is simple, when the country has many share buyers number suddenly been increasing rapidly. Consequently, these large group share investors must need to spend much time to research any kinds of company shares variations, whether when their share prices will rise up of fall down in order to achieve buying the company's shares in the lowest price and selling the company's shares in the highest price level in order to earn profit.

Basic on this reason, they must need to spend much extra time to research share prices changing behavior every day, e.g. one working person will wait to leave his/her job, after he/she can spend time to gather data to research the day's share price changing behavior after dinner. So, the working person's right time may be his/her share price market research behavior. Before he/she may spend his/her night time to go to shopping after dinner, but nowadays, he/she will fogive to do his/her shopping behavior before dinner or after dinner at hight sometime. He/she will make decision to spend much night time to turn on computer to click on share market website to research his/her share purchase choice to investigate whether his/her share price whether it rises up or falls down at the moment in order to make his/her share buying or selling decision at ever night time.

I mean the when the country has many people are share investors, their shares investment behavioral spenging time which will influence many shops lose customers at might often because the country will have many people feel need to spend night time to turn on computer or watch television to investigate share price variation. So, the country will have many people / share investors choose to stay at home in order to carry on share price variation investigation behavior, they need to listen share market update news from radios or watch the share market update news from computer or TV at home every night. Consequenly, they must reduce times to leave themselves homes at night. So, their shopping behavior also will be reduced. Because these share investors feel need to spend time to investigate share price variation news at homes which can bring economic benefits (high opportunity benefits) when they choose to forgive to leave homes to go to shopping times (opportunity cost) every night.

On conclusion, it seems that when the country has many people are share investors, then their share price investigating behavior may bring negative shopping emotion at night. Consequently, the country's any one shop may lose many customers from this share investor consumer group in behavioral economic view. Hence, when the country's share investors number had been increasing rapidly, it will influence any shops lose many customers from this share investing customer group at night frequenly in short time, even long time in behavioral economic view, because their shopping desires or shopping emotion will be brought negative feeling when they make decisions to spend much time to listen radios or watch TV or computers share price update nes at night. Hence, share market will bring negative impact to influence consumer shopping desire or negative shopping emotion in behavioral economic view.

Can technology influence human shopping behavioral change?
Nowadays, technological development has reached mature stage, whether technological mature stage may bring positive or negative shopping emotion influence to global consumers. I shall aplly internet inventin or ecommerce shopping channel tool to explain whether internet technology can bring postive or negative influence to global consumer behavior in behavioral economic view.
Internet is a good technological tool, it brings e-commerce business chance.

In fact, commonly, global has have many businessmen choose to use internet channel to carry on their products transactions between global online-buyers and their electronic websites. So, global many shoppers had begun to feel online shopping is more convenient to compare visiting shops shopping. Their shopping behaviors have been changed from internet technological tool. Global has many shoppers choose to buy any products from any overseas or local businessmen their web stores. They only need to spend time to find any businessmen their webstores to choose the most suitable products to pay visa to buy from their webstores. at homes. So, in general, global had have may shoppers had changed their shopping behaviors from visiting shops to visiting webstores at homes often.

So, it seems that internet technological tool had influenced global many shops disappear, but internet webstores will be replaced their actual shops on streets. Some of businessmen either they choose webstores to replace shops or choose websotes and shops both or still keep shops only. Hence, internet tool influences global businessmen have three kinds of products sale channels to let globa local and overseas consumers to choose how to buy their products.

However, in fact, many of global shoppers, youngers and olders had begun to accept to buy any products from webstores. They feel to spend time to leave homes to visit shops , their shopping behaviors will be wasted time to not essential part to their daily lives. Hence, since internet technological invention, it had changed many consumers their traditional visiting shops shopping habit to change to buying products from webstores channel.

However, on the one hand, internet creates webstores ecommerce shopping channel to let global many consumers do not need to leave homes to go to shopping. It brings negative visiting shops shopping emotion to global general consumers nowadays. But on the other hand, it also brings positive visiting internet webstores shopping emotion to global general consumer nowadays. So, it seems that global many consumers feel that they often do not need to spend much time to go out shopping. Many global consumers feel convenient and enjoy to choose any products to buy from different internet webstores, when the online buyer chooses the most suitable product, he she only needs to pay visa card to buy the product from the online seller's webstore conveniently at home.

Hence, online shopping can bring economic benefit to online buyers, e.g. avoiding walking time or spending transport fare to visit the shop to go to shopping, shortening or reducing shopping time to do another important matter.

On conclusion, global many consumers began feel online shopping can bring more economic benefits on shortening shopping time, avoiding transport fare spending aspect. So, online shopping will be popular shopping behavior for future long time. It may encourage global many shoppers can make rapid shopping decision in short time in order to carry on any products buying transaction to global any one online shopper in short time easily in behavioral economic view. So, global many businessmen had begun to build themselves one attraction webstore in order to persuade different countries consumers to choose to click themselves webstores from internet channel to buy any kinds of products in short time easily.

So, internet technology had changed consumers traditional shopping behaviors to build positive online shopping emotion as well as raise online sellers' any products sale chance easily in behavioral economic view.

Why and how human behavior may influence the country's economic growth or recession?

When one country has many people choose to do the same matter for one period, whether their behavior may influence the country's pvera; economic growth or recession . I shall attempt to indicate cases toexplain their relationship as below:

For flowing rubblish behavioral case example, do you feel that when the country has many people often flow rubblish on the streets, instead of their flowing rubblish behavior may bring streets dirty? But, their flowing rubblish behavior may explain that this country has people may have enough money to buy food to ear, or enough cloths to wear, enough bottles of water to drink, even they may have enough money to buy new television, radio, refrigeraters , washing machines, desktops or laptops electronic home products from old to new to use in order to satisfy their living needs. So, when they flow old electronic home products, their flowing old home electronic products behaviors may seem that they have enough money to buy other new home electronic products to replace old home electronic products to use at homes.

However, it seems thaat this country ought have many people have jobs to do. So, many of them, they can easy to make purchase decison to flow any old home electronic products and buy any new home electronic products to use . Because this country has many people have jobs to do. So, they can often not use old home electonic products to become rubblishs to flow on streets after they had bought any kinds of new home electronic homes.

In fact, it also implies that this country's economy grows rapidly. So, many businesses can glow up rapdly. When they expanded their businesses, they must need to increase employees number in order to let they help themselves to raise productivity or serve their clients absolutely. So, when the country has many businesses can grow up, it seems that its economy must be better or it is improved to compare past. Due to many different kinds of home electronic products had been often bought to use by this country people in this period. So, this country's any streets can be observed that expensive electronic home products were flowed on streets anywhere. then, this country will have many electronic home products sellers can sell their home electronic products very easily. When this country has many people can find any kinds of jobs to do easily. So, due to unemploymen rate had been decreasing.

In behavioral economic view, as this many electronic home products rubblish country case, we can observe this country may have many people have jobs to do. So, consumption number has been increased long time. So, cheap food, or expensive home electronic products may be rubblish on any streets. This country's people , their flowing rubblish behaviors may be explained that many of people have enough jobs to do, so they have ability to buy any good taste food to eat or buy any kinds of expensive electronic home products to use. So, this country's economy may be improved for this long period. So, in behavioral economic view, when this country can have many electronic home products rubblishs are flowed on anywherer in streets frequently. It seems that this country will have many people have jobs to do, so it causes they often change old home electronic products or replaced them easily, when they have enough income to spend to buy any kinds of new home electronic products to use at homes easily. Moreover, their flowing old electronic home products behaviors also indicate that this country has many people their salaries may be increased in possible from their emplyers. When this country can have many different kinds of home electornic products are sold. It means that this country's electronic home products needs or demand had been increasing, due to many people have jobs to do and income increases to excite their living of needs also improve. Consequently, this country may seem have better economic improvement. We can observe from this country's electronic home products rubblish increasing income in theis period.

On conclusion, this country ought experience economic growth at this period. So, " flowing expensive electronic home rubblish increasing number

" may seem that this country's economic growth is rapidly in this period, due to many people have jobs to do as well as salaries increase in this period.

Technology how impacts human behavior changing?
Technology how influences human behavior to bring changing? For example, online share purchase and sale transaction from smart phone brings share investor can do share buying or selling transation in any where and any time conveniently, non manual driving auto vehicle, bring car owner feels comfortable and spends free time to do other matter, e.g. reading, listening mucis in himself or herself car freely. electrical energy vehicle can help car owner to reduce air polluton and it can brings the drivers do not feel drive long time in any journeys in order to avoid air pollution for environmental protection responsible car drivers in our societies. Thus, they will drive long time in any journeys when they can drive electronic energy cars to replace oil energy cars.

However, online technology can also bring consumers can choose to stay at homes to buy any things from seller individual online webstore conveniently. Such as online technology can bring shoppers do not need to spend much time to visit shops to buy any things. They can choose any kinds of products from any online sellers individual online webstores conveniently at homes. Online technology excite busy consumers can make purchase decision easily as well as it can help online sellers sell any kinds of products from internet easily.

In behavioral economic view, technology can change human behavior to be improved, it can let human feels comfortable, more free time ro use, rapid making any decisions, such as apply smart phones to make share purchase or sale transaction decision, online shopping decision, even travelling any where decision in short time, when the traveller finds the most cheap hotel accommodation room price and air ticket price frm any travel agent online tourism webstore, then the potential travel customer can follow the online hotel accommodation price and air ticket price data to make decision when to buy the air ticket from the airline travel agent or make decision when to prebook which hotel accommodation room to go to the country to travel from online travel agent tourism webstores. So, technology can encourage global any country travelers to make anywhere to trvel rapidly. If the traveler can find the country's general hotel rooms and airline tickets prices had been decreasing more sightly. The traveler may make travel decision to choose the country to travel in short time, then he/she can prebook the country;s any hotel room and airline ticket to pay by visa fraom the country's any hotel and airline travel agent webstores., before one week, even one month or more easily. Hence, online technology can also encourage traveler individual frequent travel times to be increased, due to global travelers can find any hotel rooms and airline tickets prices from internet conveniently at homes. They do not need to spend time to visit any airline travel agent to enquire travel choice country's hotel rooms prices and airline ticket prices. They can compare global travel of countries choices ' all hotels rooms and airline agents air tickets prices to make prebook airline seat and hotel room decision before one week, one month even six months early.

On conclusion, online technology can encourage global travelers can make travelling any where and when traveling time desicions easily. It can excite tourism industry develops in long time. Also, such as electricity cars invention can encourage environment protection car owners do car purchase decision easily, because they can choose to drive electronic energy cars to replace oil energy cars in order to avoid air pollution occurs easily. So, electronic cars can increase electronic car purchasrs number, due to many of environmental protection attitude of car owners can choose to drive electricity cars to bring air cleans, even non -manual driving cars can encourage lazy driving and free time driving car owners to choose to buy non-manual (artificial intelligent) cars to drive , because they can spend much free time to read, listen music or do any matters in themselves cars, they do not need to drive cars, robotic (AI) auto driving machine is such one non-manual driver to help them to drive themselves cars confidently. So, non-manual driving cars can attract lazy and enjoying free time driving car owners to choose to buy to replace traditional manual cars to drive easily. Moreover, online share transaction can help any share investors to make share buying and selling decision in short time easily. When they can apply smart phones technological tool to carry on share buying and selling activities easily. They can observe any share rising or falling price suitation from smart phones in any where any any time easily. So, smart phone technology can help global any shareholders to make share purchase and sale transaction easily. So, technology can encourage human makes decision in short time rapidly.

How and why employees behaviors may influence economy development?

In behavioral economy view,I believe the country's any organizational employees behavior may bring indirect relationship to influence the country's long term economic development. I shall indicate past manufacture industry social development period to explain their relationship. For many countries' past business activities had belonged to manufacturing industry, such as US, UK past before 1980 year, it focused on steel manufacturing and steel manufacturing related machine products. So, US, Uk developed countries manufacturing industries may be past main country's economic income sources. I assume US , UK past had one million number different kinds of industries. They ought had about seven houndred thousand number organizational businesses were belonged to manufactured industry. They may include:

Steel manufacturing and steel related machine manufacturing, e.g. vehicle manufacturing, home appliances, e.g. washing machine, television, radio, refrigerate cooler, heater, air condition etc. different kinds of different kinds of steel -related manufacturing machine, they were manufactured from US, UK steel machine manufacturers. So, US, Uk the other three hundred thousand number industry may be general service industry, e.g. hotel service, restaurent, cinema, public transport service, tourism lesiure , wine bar, supermarket etc. different kinds of non-manufacturing industries business organizations were operated in UK, US past before 1980 year.

So, in UK, US developed countries industry development history, they ought have high percentage of businesses belonged to steel related manufacturing machine and steel products. Also, in the past before 1980 year, US, Uk business employers , they employed many workers are manufacturing workers. They needed to spend long time to work in factories. They were skillful workers, and they are trained to manufacturing cars, washing machine, television, heater, etc. even steel itself different kinds of steel related products to prepare to deliver to their shops to sell to US, Uk local or overseas clients.

So, I believe that past UK, US ought employ many employees, they belonged to skillful manufacturing workers, manufacture increasing steel machine or steel related machine number of products rapidly daily. So, if UK, US had had many of these manufacturing factories owned high skillful workers, then their manufacturing steel-related machine or steel both kinds of products number must be influenced to raise rapidly. Consequently, their steel machine manufacturing products would been exported to overseas or would been sold to local both markets , they may be influenced to raise sale number. They (these manufacturing workers) needed to be trained to know how to manufactur these different kinds of machine products in the efficient teams and they ought to be trained to raise their efficiencies in order to shorten time to manufacturing many kinds of steel related manufacturing machine or steel itself products rapidly. So , if their efficiencies and manufacturing performance was improved, these US, UK any one manufacturing worker and their teams ought achieve raising productivities significantly.

Hence, when past UK, US manufacturing industry development period, if these two countries' any manufacturing factories could have many manufacturing workers could be trained to be skillful and proficient manufacturing workers. Then, in past every day to these factories workers, they ought help their steel or steel related manufacturing employers to raise any kinds of machine or steel products number in every team. So, when past in the manufacturing industry development, US, UK could have many factories' manufacturing workers themselves steel or steel related machine products manufacturing skill could be trained to to improve to any kinds of these machine or steel manufacuring products quality as well as their products number could be influenced to raise by themselves skillful improvement significantly every day.

Then, what would be influenced to occur to past UK, US manufacturing industry period? In behavioral economic view, when these two manufacturing industry developed countries, such as UK, US , if they had many factories workers can be trained to improve their skill in order to achieve any kinds of steel or steel-related machine products quality could be improved as well as products manufacturing number could be also increased absolutely.

In consequence, past UK and US both countries ought increase themselves any kinds of steel and steel related machine products number to be supplied to themselves local shops to let local clients to choose any one kind of machine manufacturing products to buy easily as well as they could also export to supply overseas any countries to buy their different kinds of steel or steel related machine products to let overseas steel or steel related manufacturing machine product buyers, they can have many of these different kinds of these steel or steel-related different kinds of manufacturing machine from UK and UK these both countries easily to compare other countries.

On conclusion, I believe that past US, and UK macro manufacturing industry income GDP would increase significantly. So, they would have good economic growth performance because when many of these manufacturing workers themselves manufacturing effort could be improved. So, it explained when employees manufacturing abilities can influence economic growth indirectly.

Robots invention whether they can help organizations to raise efficiencies or inefficiencies?

In behavioral economic view, in any organizations, when the organization hopes its worker teams can raise efficiencies , the organization may choose to increase more workers number and/or it can provide training to improve these workets themselves skills in order to raise their efficiencies. For one warehouse example, when the warehouse increases many goods , they are needed to delivered these goods from the shelves to the delivering destination locations. If this warehouse supervisors feel these workers themselves goods delivery speeds are slow, which is possible due to this warehouse's workers number is not enough. So, this warehouse supervisor ought increase workers number in order to increase their goods delivery speed in order to deliver goods from the shelves to every indicated goods delivery destination in order to let any one lorry driver can transport the right kinds of goods and ensure the accurate goods number to transport to any one client home rapidly.

However, if this warehouse supervisor planed to buy several warehouse goods delivery robots to assist these warehouse workers to find the right kinds of goods from shelves and then deliver to the right destination location in the warehouse. So, these warehouse orkers can concentrate on counting the accurate goods number and ensuring the right kinds of goods in order to prepare to let lorry drivers to transport these goods to these goods of buyers themselvers homes rapidly. Consequently, in the first step, robots can concentrate on finding th right goods from shelves and delivers them to the right goods transportation of location destination. Then, in the second step, these warehouse workers can concentrate on counting the accurate goods number and ensuring the right kinds of goods in order to prepare to put them to the lorry. Consequently, when warehouse robots and warehouse workers can cooperate to work together, the most important, robots, can deal on finding the right kinds of goods and deal on delivering the accurate number of goods of job duty as well as these warehouse workers can only concentrte on counting the right kinds of goods number in order to avoid it has none any mistake of wrong kinds of goods and inaccurate goods of delivery number to be transported to the lorry and to deliver to any one buyer's home.

So, it seems that warehouse robots ought help any one warehouse worker to raise himself efficiency and avoid goods delivery of mistake occurrence easily as well as their help to warehouse workers that can let any one goods buyer feels their goods can be delivered to their homes rapidly. Moreover, warehouse robots can also help these warehouse workers to raise efficiencies because warehouse robots can help them to shorten goods delivery time between any one shelf and any one goods delivery destination of location in the warehuse because robots may help them to find the right kinds of goods from the right shelf in the short time. So, any one worker does not need to spend long time to seek anywhere is the right shelf location for the kind of goods when the kind of goods are needed to deliver to the buyer's home from lorry. Warehouse robots can help them to do this aspect of " finding the goods from the right shelf in short time job duty". So, any one warehouse worker only needed tospend less time to do the counting of any right kind of goods number and ensuring the right kind of goods job duty. Consequently, this warehouse 's any one worker, his any one kind of goods delivery time may be reduced, because robots' assistance and they may have more confidence to avoid mistake to deliver the wrong number of goods and/or the wrong kind of goods to any one goods buyer's home.

On conclusion, it seems that warehouse robots ought may help any one warehouse worker to raise efficiency for any one team in the warehouse as well as the warehouse any one supervisor does not need to spend much time to observe any one worker individual performance for " goods delivery job duty aspect" because their goods delivery job duty that had been replaced to do by these several warehouse robots. Robots can achieve the more accurate of right kinds of goods and the right number of goods delviery job performance to compare any one of human warehouse worker themselves right kinds of goods of delivery and right number of goods of delivery job performance. So, when robots can participate to cooperate with this warehouse's any one worker to do their goods of delivery job duty in this warehouse every day. Then, robots can raies any one of supervisor individual confidence in order to let they do not need to spend time to observe any one of worker individual whose goods of delivery job performane. They can concentrate on supervising any one worker whose goods transport to lorry in the final step in order to avoid to deliver wrong goods number and / or wrong kind of goods to any one goods buyer's home every day. Consequently, this warehouse's overall teams of their delviery of goods performance many be improved by robotss' participatin to goods of delivery task as well as this warehouse's oveall teams themselves efficiencies may be influenced to raise by robots' goods of delivery task participation.

Why social behavior may influence organizational strategy needs to be changed ?

Why any organizations need to know whether nowadays social behaivor how has been changing in order to implement the kind of the most right strategy to achieve the profit aim pursue in possible. I shall indicate nowadays ecommerce or online, customer shopping behavior to explain above question concerns they ought have close relationship between social behavior and organizational strategic choice or organizational behavioral changing need.

On nowadays ecommerce business, or online shopping model, this kind of shopping model in global many young and old age consumers like to apply internet tool to choose any country sellers website stores in order to stay at home to buy any kinds of products from themselves webstores in global societies.

In fact, online shopping model had been popular for long time above to twenty years. Most of global sellers will make decision to design themselves webstores in order to attract global many online buyers to choose to buy their products from themselves webstores. So, it seems that social consumers purchase behaviors had been changed to online shopping from internet invention.

Hence, social consumers purchase behavioral changes may influence any organizations' strategies need to be changed from visiting shops purchase strategy model to online purchase strategy model, if the seller still concentrate on concentrate on considerate how to design itelf , but neglects to considerate how to design itself webstore, e.g. how to design attract product photos to put on itself webstore, how to arrange sale price information location to be putted on webstore and visa card payment location on itself webstore in order to let any one online buyer can feel very easier to buy itself any kinds of products from itself webstore. Then, its potential online buyers will be influenced to increase number when they can find this online seller itself any kinds of products photes and every kinds of product sale price information and visa card payment channel locations easily from itself webstore.

So, it implies that nowadays any one seller ought need to design one webstore to let any one online overseas and domestic consumers can have chance to click itself webstore to choose any one kind of product to buy conveniently when he/she does not hope to leave him/her home to go to shop, because nowadays social shopping behaviors had been influenced to change when internet invention, them it gives another online purchase method to replace visiting shops purchase method to global any one buyer in nowadays societies.

So, if nowadays any one seller still concentrate on how to design itself shop display in order to put any kinds of product on shelf in order to let any one visiting shop customer to find the kind of product to buy, but it neglects to change to choose to pursue another new technological shopping method, such as webstore purchase method in order to implement effective strategy to design the most right webstore as well as in order to attract global overseas and local consumers to find itself webstore easily from website and find its any one kind of product phots and sale price and visa card payment button in order to choose to buy itself any kinds of products in the short time. Consequently I believe that the seller will lose many customers from overseas and local when its other same or similar product sellers choose to design themselves webstores in order to let global any one product buyer can buy themselves any one kind of product when they can pay visa card to buy their products from them webstores conveniently when they stay at home habitly. Then, the seller will lose many global potential customers in long time.

On conclusion, in behavioral economic view, any consumer behavioral social changing, which will influence any in order to avoid customers number loses significantly . In future time, organizations need to make rapid decision in order to implement the most reasonable and the most useful strategy in order to avoid global potential customers number reduces or lose them in long time. So, social behavioral changing environment ought influence any global organizations need to decide how to change themselves strategies in order to avoid customers loses significantly in future time.

How and why human behavior may influence economic growth or recession?

May ourselves daily behaviors influence our global societial continue economic growth or recession? Do they have cause and effect close relationship between human behaviors and global economic growth or recession? I shall apply behavioral economic theory to analyze and explain whether ourselves daily behaviors and our global societial economic growth or recession which have close cause and effect relationship as below:

Every country itself economic development must depend on any business activities, otherwise, any kinds of business activities must need ourselves business activities or behaviors in order to achieve any business activities as well as achieve the country's overall economic development in macro view. However, any country's overall business activites or behaviors which must depend on any kinds of individual businessmen, themselves employees daily working behavior or activity or performance in order to help them to attract or increase many clients number to acieve " earning profit" aim. So, it seems that any individual business, itself overall every department individual working behavior is one main factor to influence the company's overall business performance.

For agricultural fruit and meat food farming industry example, such as New Zealand is a farming main target industry country. It had had many New Zealanders were daily themselves own farming businesses for many years. Their farming businesses include growing fruit, sheep, cow, pig pork, meat etc. food sale business. If the New Zealand farmer owned a large size farming land, then he will choose either growing fruit or feeding sheeps, pigs, cows to be meat to to transport to New Zealand supermarkets to help them to sell to their farmers meet to New Zealanders in order to earn profit. Thus, if the New Zealand farmer owned large size of farming lands, then he needs to employ many farming employees (farming workers) to help him to carry on farming business daily tasks, e.g. picking up friuts, feeding pigs, cows, sheeps to eat food daily. These daily farming jobs are very important to influence this New Zealand farmer's meats or fruits sale number whether they can be easy or diffcult to sell in New Zealand supermarkets , if these farming workers can own encough farming knowledge or skill to know how to pick up fruits method and make judgement to know whether it is right time to pick up the kind of fruits from the trees , as well as know how feed this pigs, sheeps, cows to eat food in order to let they are better health. Consequently, their farming behaviors which can let these animals can provide the best taste and enough meat from these animals to let New Zealander to buy to eat from New Zealand any one supermarket. Even these New Zealand farming workers can know whether the kinds of fruits, e.g. oranges, apples, gapes etc. fruits whether they ought be picked up from the trees at the right time. Consequently, they can make judgement to decide to pick up any kinds of the best taste fruits to let any one New Zealander to buy to eat from any one supermarket in New Zealand. Otherwise, if they do not make judegement to know whether the kind of fruit ought not be picked up because they still need longer time to continue grow up to increase fruit size and better taste from the trees in order to let any one fruit buyer can feel better taste when they eat this kind of fruit later. If they can buy this kind of fruit to eat later, then this New Zealand farmer's his fruit buyers can buy the best taste of this kind of fruit to eat from an yone supermarket in New Zealand. Consequently, many New Zealand supermarkets will choose to buy any kinds of fruits from this farmer fruit supplier when they feel this farmer's fruits can provide more better taste fruits to compare other farmers' fruits.

Thus, due to New Zealand is one farming main income source country. It's any kinds of fruits and meats need to be export to overseas to sell , instead of local sale. It's GDP percent is very high to whole country 's overall income source. So, any one New Zealand farmer individual and any one farming worker individual working behavior will influence its economy whether it is influenced to grow or recession possible. Moreover, it also seems that farming workers' farming knowledge and skill will influence themselves farming daily activities to achieve the aim of the number of increase or decrease to any kinds of fruits whether they are better taste or the number of increase of decrease to any kinds of meats whether they are better taste to supply to any one New Zealand fruit or meat buyers to eat from any one New Zealand supermarket. So, it implies that any one New Zealand farming worker individual farming behavior may influence any kinds of fruits or any kinds of meat taste because they are transported to any one supermarket to sell in New Zealand.

Consequently, if New Zealans had many farmers can teach god farming knowledge and skill to let their any one farming workers know how to decide judgement to decide when it is right time to pick up any kinds of fruits from trees , or how to grow them on soil in order to let they can grow rapidly. Then, many different kinds of fruits can be provided to let any one New Zealanders can eat the best taste of fruits when their fruits are supplied to any one New Zealand supermarkets. Even, if they knew how to feed foods to pigs, cows, sheeps to eat daily. Then they can be more health and they can provide the best taste of meats to let any one New Zealanders can buy their meats from any one New Zealand supermarkets. Moreover, their fruits and meats can be transported to overseas to let any one country fruits or meats buyers can choose any kinds of New Zealand meats and fruits to buy to eat from themselves countries supermarkets. Then, many overseas fruit and meat buyers will perfer to choose New Zealand any kinds of fruits or meats to buy to compare other countries fruits or meats to buy when they go to any one local supermarkets.

On conclusion, it seems that New Zealand farming workers themselves farming behavior may influence their farming employers any kinds of fruits or meats sale number and income because their farming task behaviors must influence whether their fruits or meats taste are the better taste or worse taste to compare their other local farmers (the farmer competitors) whose fruits or meats taste. If tthe farmer's any one farming worker can be trained to learn how to know to feed animals skill and when is the most right time to pick up any kinds of fruits from trees or how to grow them on the soil methods. Due to these farming worker individual farming behavior may influence his different finds of fruits and meats sale number to be increase or decrease, so these any one New Zealand farmer must need to depend on any one farming worker whose farming working methods, if their farming working behaviors can be the best to influence any kinds of fruits to grow rapid or any kinds of pigs, cows, sheeps animals grow up rapidly , then their sale number may be increase significantly and their taste can be improved to let any New Zealand or overseas meat or fruit buyer to buy to eat to feel from any one New Zealand or overseas supermarkets, then New Zealand's agriculture industry must be influenced to increase. In the world, any one fruit or meat buyer must choose to buy New Zealand's fruit and meat to eat in prefer to compare other countries' fruits and meats. So, New Zealand's GDP may be influenced to raise from any one New Zealand farming worker individual farming working behaviors.

Reasons why human behavior may influence economic recession or growth?

Can ourselves daily behaviors or activies influence ourselves countries' economic growth or recession? I shall attempt to explain the reasons why they have direct or indirect relationship between human behavior and economy growth or recession as below:

I shall indicate environment pollition case to attempt to explain above question. Our societies had been experiencing servious environment pollution challenge. However, environment pollution , such as air pollution is caused by air planes and vehicles emission by air planes and vehicles emission as well as water pollution is caused by plastic rubblish, or dirty water or oil or gas chemical material, these both kinds of pollution ought may bring economic recession and this both kinds of pollution are caused by human ourselves daily foolish activities.

I believe human behavior and economy and pollution which have cause and effect relationship. I shall analyze this environment pollution case to explain why they have case and effect relationship between human foolish behavior and environment pollution and economic recession as below:

When global societies had many people like to buy cars to drive to bring emission to fresh air on the roads as well as many manufacturing factories will bring emission to pollute fresh air in their manufacturing processes. Factories and cars will bring air pollution , due to factories need to pollute fresh air in order to manufacture many products and car owners need to drive their cars to go to offices or leisure places. Their cars will also bring emisson to pollute fresh air. On consequence, car owners themselves frequent driving behaviors and factory workers themselves frequent manufacturing behaviors may bring environment pollution. Technology or human behavior whether may influence economic growth or recession. Moreover, air planes also brings emission to pollute air when they are flying in sky. Also, when ships bring oil pollution or sea plastic rubblishs bring pollution to global oceans.

In fact, manufactuers and cars owners, such as factories workers manufacturing behaviours ans car owners driving behaviors and pilots driving air planes flying behaviors and ships transport behaviors, which may cause plastic rubblish, oil or gas emission to sky or sea or on the road to cause ocean and air pollution is serious. However, human ourselves need to buy cars to drive to satisfy ourselves driving leisure or enjoyment, travelers need to catch air planes to travel to enjoy leisure needs, factories workers need help factories to manufacture many products to sell to customers to satisfy their using needs. oil exploration needs to find lands to explore new oil lands.

All of these business and leisure activites may bring serious air and water pollution. However, due to serious air and water pollution will bring earth warming challenge , such as some countries temperature will be influences to rise up to 40 degree or higher br earth warming. However, earth warming is caused by air and ocean pollution. Pollution must be caused by human ourselves, driving cars leisure and factories manufacturing business activities. Hence, if human decided to continue to do these foolish behaviors, we only pursue to manufacture different kinds of industrial products or drive cars to enjoy leisure aims, but we also neglect ourselves behaviors may bring environment pollution. Then, earth warming or earth temperature will be influenced to rise up absolutely in long term. Moreover, if our future earth will be influenced to bring serious high temperature effect by human ourselves these foolish behaviors.

On consequencey, warth warming will bring serious economic losses in possible because when ourselves earth temperature had been influenced to rise up to 40 degree or high. Ourselves health will be caused poor, due to we will feel difficult breath, we must need often tried and hard to work, due to our nervous and health will be influenced to poor by pollution and earth warming effect. Also, we need to pay more money to see doctors when we had long life. Then, our societies will lose may strong labors to help manufacturers to work, e.g. factories will reduce workers number to help manufacturers to produce more different kinds of products, due to workers health is general poor. Due to lacking enough workers to manufacture products, our societies will begin to reduce enough supply number of products to sell to global consumers to satisfy their use needs.

On conclusion, in behaviroal economic view, our societies will lose many labors due to their bodies are not health by air and water pollution. Global economic and business activities will be influenced to worse by global workers reducing number reason. So, economic recession will begin to occur in possible when pollution reaches the serious level.

CHAPTER FIVE

How (AI) technology impacts energy industry development

How (AI) technology impacts food consumers
and food manufacturers food eating habits
or attitudes to avoid wastage

Can artificial intelligence impact food consumers' eating habits to be influenced to change ? Future (AI) technology (big data gathering tool) can be used to gather data concerns to supervise or manage or control these below food consumers and food manufacturers' food waste or food loss behaviours in order to find the main reasons to cause their food waste or loss wastage behaviours in order to achieve to prevent or avoid their wastage behaviours occurrence again more easily. I shall explain to these aspects as below, they include :

On (AI) auto-supervised food consumer individual food waste behavioural aspect:

Firstly, for the original food wastage supervised, the original food which included food in unopened packages behaviours, which was thrown away because it passed the expiration date including products to like cheese, yogurts and other daily products, loose fruits and vegetables which became rotten and was never used. (AI) technology can follow these waste food gather number from different countries' supermarkets, food stores to gather waste food number in order to carry statistic analysis to find the reasons why these kinds of original food, cheese, yogurts, fruit and vegetable wastage number has increase to every month in order to attempt to find the reasons to cause wastage food behaviours , it is either caused by either food manufacturers' food losses (good manufacturing process negligent factor) cause or food consumers' food eating habits cause in order to find the solution methods to change their wrong food loss or waste influential behaviours to the food manufacturers as well as the wrong food habits or attitudes to the food household consumers more easily and accurately.

Secondly, for another kind of wastage food is partly used food supervised, the food which could have been opened or started, but was never finished. (AI) data gathering tool can attempt to follow different countries' food rubbish to gather the number data to find how much rubbish number is belonged to the country's wastage food is partly used food or the food which could have been opened or started, but was never finished to find the main reasons (factors) why they caused those kind of food wastage number is increased from food consumers; eating habits or what the reasons (factors) caused their number is decreased the country's food consumers' eating habits in order to find the most effective or accurate methods to solve this kind of food wastage behaviours from the country's food consumers.

Thirdly, for the another kind of food wastage is leftover supervised, which consist of food left or the plates or were cooked in big amounts which ended is not being eaten. (AI) technology big data gathering tool can gather global these kind of food waste number concerns every householder's food left on plates or were cooked in big amounts to every country, but not being eaten number from their rubbish.

TO attempt to find what factors(reasons) influence their food habits to do food left on the plates or were cooked in big amounts , which are nor being eaten food habits. SO, it can follow this kind of global food wastage increasing or decreasing number every month statist data to attempt find what factors influence this kind of food wastage to household food consumers to be either decreased or what factors influence this kind of food wastage number to be increased to conclude the more accurate food behavioural wastage judgement for this kind of food wastage habits to every country household food consumers, e.g. life habitual factor, food price factor, food perishable factor, climate influence factor etc. different kinds of external factors to cause every country's household food wastage behaviours.

Finally, the final kind of food wastage is that preparation residues, (vegetable peels, egg shells) supervised, this kind of food wastage could potentially be still used and not known away by global every householder food consumers, they can not be avoided to waste before cooling, due to the householder feels these foods are not fresh to eat. So, the householder chooses not to cook it to eat.

However, (AI) technology can gather data concerns different countries' householder fresh food purchasing habits ,e.g. per week or per twice week or per day fresh food purchasing frequently and fresh food purchasing number, such as vegetable peels etc. fresh food wastage rubbish number in order to find what the main factors (reasons) is (are) to cause the next month fresh food wastage number to be increased or decreased to every country householders in order to conclude the more accurate or reasonable wrong fresh food wastage habitual behaviours to cause different countries' fresh food householders' fresh food wastage behaviours habitually.

In conclusion, basing on above evidences, I can explain why future (AI) technological big data gathering tool can be applied to find solutions to avoid that food consumers to do food wastage behaviours habitually. It also explain why food wastage education method is only knowledge concept to educate to let public to know. In fact, food consumers can choose either do or not do to avoid food wastage in their eating habits daily. Otherwise, (AI) big data fathering tool can be applied to attempt to gather global householders (food consumers) their daily eating habitual data in order to achieve the more accurate and predictive householders (food consumers) their eating habits or eating behaviours analysis and concludes the most efficient and effective solutions to avoid global food wastage number to be raised to every country household food consumers. So, (AI) technology can impact global householders (food consumers) eating or food habits to be improved more better to compare education method.

On (AI) auto-supervised food manufacturer individual food loss behavioural aspect:

How (AI) technology changes food manufacturers cause food loss in their food manufacturing processes, I shall indicate as below:

How to apply (AI) technology to avoid vegetable, fresh fruit loss to global farmers' fresh vegetable , fruit excessive wastage loss increasing number when their crops growth process in global agricultural sector? (AI) will enable significant and valuable new solutions to avoid fresh crops, fruit, rice, vegetable food loss in their growing or irrigation process.

The internet of things (OIT) will assist (IA) in future intelligent agricultural systems, fuelled by large volumes of data acquired from images, videos and IOT sensors. For example, it be applied to water and sprays in agricultural sector. (AI) is smoothing the way for new levels of optimisation on our farms and across all horticultural activities. The automated irrigation systems are getting and the transporting of water to specific places. It is based on the real-time needs of plants. Moreover, (AI) techniques using IOT and sensors to analyse what's happening across many hectares of farming land in real time will enable improvements in predictive modelling.

Farmers will be able to check the advantages of specific phenotypes , or traits in certain growing over time . Predictive modelling will also help them forecast pest resurgences, dramatically preventing yield losses and reducing farmers' dependence on chemical pesticides to let vegetable, fruit, crop can be grown healthy.

For the university of Waikoto , NZ example, researchers are applying machine learning to near infra-red images of soil, meaning the soil does not have to be sent to the lab. This will enable farmers to apply fertilisers much more efficiently. Moreover, robots will be developed to roam between strains of needs. These bots are high enough that do not damage the soil, and because they release herbicides only onto the weeds. They are also doing more environmental protection behaviours. Many uses of (AI) in agriculture are focused on reducing the biological and ecological damage caused by inefficient use of pesticides.

For meet waste loss reducing aspect, (AI) technology can be applied to animal health monitoring . It can also be used to improve efficiencies in livestock management by optimising feeding and dispensing of medication. The (AI) technology can constantly monitor livestock , e.g. pigs, cows sheep animals movements, eating patterns and health and immediately flag animals that are showing unusual behaviour or reduced welling. They can then be treated quickly before they spread infection. So, farmers benefit is from cost reduction through more targeted use of antibiotics when also improving the treatment of livestock.

In the simplest terms, images are constantly captured and pre-processed through detection for frequency and density to livestock eating animals' eating behaviours and living and health conditions in order to provide health pork, beef, sheep meet to consumers to eat.

However, (AI) can be applied to crop seed or fruit improved growing or better irrigation aspect, for New Zealand kiwifruit agricultural irrigation case, yield well ahead of scheduled harvests. New Zealand kiwifruit growers have had to manually count fruit over certain areas and then to achieve the more accurate kiwifruit supplying number of consumers' demanding number scheduled harvests to satisfy New Zealand itself country's kiwifruit consumers' needs , even overseas kiwifruit consumers' needs. The agricultural sector would not know until the kiwifruit product hit supermarket shelves whether its spot sampling had been correct. Any miscalculation could cause kiwifruit waste loss. For example, if NZ kiwifruit farmers predict China kiwifruit consumer number will be on million kiwifruit consumer number in this year. However, they miscalculate the wrong kiwifruit supplying number either their needs are lesser. Then, it will occur shortage kiwifruit number to export to Chinese kiwifruit consumers in this year or their supplying export number are more, then it will occur excess kiwifruit number to Chinese kiwifruit consumers. So, (AI) technology can help NZ kiwifruit farmers to predict every country's kiwifruit needs in order to supply the enough kiwifruit number to every countries' supermarkets or fruit stores to sell. SO, it won't cause NZ kiwifruit excessive or shortage challenges occur more easily.

Hence, (AI) enabled technological tools can observant or supervise every countries' fruit consumers' eating habits to predict whether how many fruit number that they will need to eat every year more accurate. It is as simple as a smartphone to video along on trailers can help provide better estimates. The device videos , the orchard on –the-go and can then produce global fruit consumers' fruit eating habits to predict their fruit consumption behaviours more accurately in every year. From these video-based machine learning systems can detect more better and therefore count seeds and fruit months in advance. So, having these (AI) predictive crop or seeds growing number technology to predict whether is enough insights in advance would also enable harvesters to undertake section-based optimisation, improve food safety and direct fertiliser to specific locations. Global faming suppliers can better manage their crop , fruit seeds, vegetable seeds growing process and time to control or predict when they can be grown to sell when it can reaches the mature stage , even meat pricing and revenue forecasting with supermarkets or food or fruit store retailers accurately book shipping logistics and storage and reducing waste.

So, key (AI) technologies will extreme impact agriculture to change farmers' vegetable, fruit, tomato, potato, crop, and livestock animals feeding methods or behaviours to be improved better by machine learning, drones, computer vision. IOT robotics, satellite , data influence.

How to putting (AI) work in the vineyard for grape fruit growing better? For Lincoln Agri. Tech. a research and development company owned by Lincoln university , NZ case example, it is developing an (AI) solution which can make early season predictions of vineyard harvests. (AI) technology can help NZ grape growers and wineries to predict their grape yield each year. SO, (AI) technology can help them to do grape yield prediction work. A large number of manual workers do sample grape bunches work. SO, (AI) technology is working on creating a system that instead uses electronic sensors to accurately count grapes for NZ grape fruit farmers. The sensors will capture and analyse grape bunches within individual rows, and access the number, sizes and distribution, feeding these different kinds of grape number data into computer algorithms in order to predict grape yield at harvest time to calculate the different kinds of grape yield to different countries grape consumers' needs more accurately. New date will also be added to the (AI) computer system each year, leading to continuous improvements in the model's accuracy as more information is gathered under different conditions. Hence, (AI) system will enable NZ grape growers to accurately access differences in yield , not only between regions or vineyards, but also blocks and rows. Over the long term, site-specific grape yield prediction will help reduce costs by enabling better planning both in the vineyard and in NZ grape market, even overseas grape market both. This (AI) technology will benefit the agricultural industry by supporting better crop or seed management, smoother processing and fruit , vegetable, crop market based on capacity to supply the more accurate number.

Global farmers can apply (AI) technology to improve agricultural water system to let crop, fruit, vegetable to grow more easily to avoid waste loss number rises. Applying on farming sensors and other data to provide farmers with daily recommendations around nitrogen application and water and effluent irrigation . It can be accessed via smartphone, take the guess-work out of interpreting the large amounts of data farmers need to consider before making an irrigation decision.

(AI) agricultural water irrigation computer system can expand into nitrogen application management and water irrigation scheduling. Optimising the amount and timing of effluent are key components of ensuring farm sustainability and resource consent compliance, minimising leaching and optimising pasture growth.

Future (AI) technology just-in-time water management can provide enough water supply to satisfy agricultural fruit, vegetable, crop etc. food irrigation need to global different farming lands more easily. In farming industry, enough fresh water irrigation need is very important to influence any fruit , vegetable, crop etc. food growing process successfully. (AI) technology can be applied to this farming land water supply aspect. It can measure when the farming land needs how much water supply to provide to the farming land's fruit, vegetable, crop growth more easily. Either when the farming land does not need water supply, or when the farming land has still have enough water in the farming underground land. For example, a Florida water company is using artificial intelligence to reduce withdrawal of water from the area aquifer in Jacksonville, USA. Tis (AI) water supply measurement system can forecast water consumption , then monitors, regulates and adjusts supply in real-time , providing a just-in0time water supply to the farming underground lane. This minimises wall production during peak hours, optimises reservoir storage, and reduces the number of pump starts required, lowering energy consumption and maintenance costs.

The (AI) water supply management system can meet the fruit, vegetable crop growing demands of these food consumers needs and reduce the need to big new wells and preserve for un-predictive water supplying need for any fruit, vegetable, crop water need on any farming lands. So, every farming land will have accurate water supplying , it won't have excessive or shortage water supply challenge to every farming lands, if the country's farmers chose to use this (AI) water supply management system.

In the future, (AI) technology advantages to be applied to food waste aspect, it can influence: assisted farming to provide enough water supply to irrigate the most accurate and measured water to every farming underground lands to let any fruit, vegetable, crops' seeds to have enough water supply to grown rapidly, reducing open-sea fishing, considered use of farming land energy supply or affordable and clean energy supply.

In the future, artificial intelligence has the potential to let any fruit vegetable, crop seeds grow up successfully. It can be used to analyse seed genetic data to create crops that can thrive and adapt in any sudden changing environment or weather in order to keep the fruit, vegetable, crop seeds can still have large adapting effort to grow up in any bad conditions. It can increase effectiveness of food supply chains through the use of (AI) technologies to drive insights that improve any fruit, vegetable, crop growing up efficiency and reduce waste in any farm. It can also give recommendations to support for farmers to choose the best decision making in order to increase in productivity. Instead of these , it can reduce the food loss in growing or manufacturing process. It can also help human to choose the healthcare diets. It includes to mine health care records to improve quality of treatments and provide better and faster health diets.

It can analyse of large scale genetic data sets to help create new types of treatment and precision medicines customised for individuals, providing expert assistance in diagnosis especially in repetitive tasks, such as analysis of images and large bodies of research information, providing immediate first line consultation to improve waiting times to see a doctor, reducing pressure on frontline staff by using robots in healthcare, speeding up the development of new drugs allowing treatments to reach whose who need them more quickly, improving learning outcomes through the analysis of data about individual learning, social and learning contexts, and personal interests, providing virtual monitors for learning by integrating modelling, social simulation and knowledge representation, providing lifelong learning companions that help the learner to adapt and build new skills throughout their lifetime. Hence, it can bring the actual life knowledge to let food manufacturers, farmers and food consumers to learn how to avoid to do food wastage or food loss behaviours in our daily life experiences. Moreover, it can help farmers , food manufacturers to learn how to optimize energy generation and reduce environmental impact through analysis of operational and environment data as well as helping food consumers or food manufacturers to find the most affordable and clean energy in efficient ways od deals when they are cooking or manufacturing foods by using (AI) agents. Even, it can improve actions to fight climate change through better modelling and analysis of large or complex data sets in order to generate better insight to help to improve the sustainable management of land resources, e.g. soils, forest, biodiversity and allow greater understanding of the impact of better farming land use choices for fruit, vegetable, crops ' seeds growth through global agricultural industry development predictive analytic and machine learning.

In conclusion, based on above different (AI) technology predictive function s, so it explains why it can replace education method to avoid or reduce future good or energy shortage challenge more easily. It is due to food consumers or food manufacturers' food waste or loss behaviours which can not be controlled to avoided to cause easily in their food manufacturing or crop growing processes as well as food consumption processes. (AI) green data revolution will create a smarter, more flexible food waste controlling system as more data is created and shared between food supply chain partners and food consumers. It can bring positive benefits to agricultural industry, such as food factory manufacturing automation, intelligent food packaging, food waste or loss risk analytics in manufacturing processes , food supply chain number forecasting, food product personalisation and new avoiding food waste or loss ways of engaging with food consumers.

Finally, I shall discuss how (AI) technology can gather data to bring food waste or food loss threat consequent message to let humans (food consumers or food manufacturers) to understand how to change their eating waste habits or food manufacturing loss behaviours more easily as below:

Future (AI) technology can gather global food manufacturing and food consumption data to conclude one accurate food system trend model to let us to influence our negative or wrong eating habits or food manufacturing behaviours to improve to more positive in order to avoid food loss or food wastage causes easily.. The food eating or manufacturing behavioural system trends model can be as below:

It includes how to consider a number of trends that will influence the food system over the coming decade, focusing on small number of " key trends" in agricultural industry and supermarket, food stores, food grocery and food manufacturing industry, fishing industry, restaurant and hotel food supply industry, these trends which focus on a number of issues across the natural environmental, social and economic influences , due to future food waste or food loss consequent causes.

Changing social norms and working practices continue to influence the frequencey and format of food consumption. Predicting how the soical media influences to the way householders make food purchasing and dining decisions to influence food consumers' food waste behaviors from online. Predicting how the widening wealth gap and aging population are altering household food shopping and eating behaviours changes. Predicting explosion of data enabled technology concerns how the amount of data is growing at an predictive rate. The offers potential for a smarter, more responsive reducing or avoiding food waste behavioral system to food consumers or food manufacturers. Predictinv how the positive changes or influences of tackling major public health and environmental challenges are caused from humans (food consumers and food manufacturers) whose food waste or food loss behaviours. Predicting food system (big data gathering method) concerns food consumers or food manufacturers' frequency of food waste or food loss behavioural data to adatp to an uncertain operating environment as well as to find the methods how to fight the risks of climate related shocks to the food shortge challenge.

Hence, the (AI) data gathering aims to achieve these missions as below:

Learning how to grow in most technology is driven a revolution in how the entire food system operates from a better understanding of land resources to automated factories and kitchens. To bring data enabled technology that will be become cheaper and more accessible all the time, but the avoiding food waste system will fully capitalise on the benefits over tehe next ten years. This avoiding food waste system will be explored to companies, households and food waste policymakers seek to make better use of data. They include as below:

(1) Increasing number of devices connected to the internet and number of social media users to learn how to avoid to do food waste or food loss behaviours daily.

(2) Decreasing the cost of data storage technology and the size od data enabled devices.

(3) The food waste avoiding system can deal with th increasing complexity and sudden changing environmental , social and economic systems to avoid the failure to respond proactively to these new challenges to bring energy, water and food shortages consequences.

(4) Increaing efforts to fight the impacts of extreme weather events, agricultural pest ranges to the food avoiding waste system interconnectedness.

(5) Understanding how to increase soil health, crop diversity, global nutrition and quality and availability of water resources.

(6) Understanding how to fight climate change, it brings significantly affect the fruit, vegetable, crop's seed growth to the improved better in agricultural industry through its impact agricultural yields, agricultural food changing prices influence, reliability of supply, food quality and food safety for ensuring long term food security and supply chain (food transportation process).

(7) Developments of the use of advanced monitoring agricultural systems to increase input efficiencies and anticipate food production risks, such as adverse weather.

(8) Skills for future food wastage or shortage challenges, learning how to fight climate change challenges.

In conclusion, (AI) preventive food wastage or shortage technological system will need to gather the data concerns when global climate and environement sudden change and finding anywhere the global most suitable farming lands are located in order to provide the right agricultural farming lands to let fruit, vegetable, crops' seed which can grow rapidly, finding anywhere the lands are located which have enough natural water supply in order to help us to solve food shortage challenge in order to irrigate enough water to farming lands to let agricultural foods grow more rapidly, and finding anywhere have enough weeds or food for pigs, cows, sheeps livestocks on the land to eat. So, above these are future (AI) preventive food wastage or shortage technological system will be invented to solve any one of these agricultural seeds growth and livestocks feeding challenges.

House quality influences householder electricity
energy consumption behavior

Can artificial intelligence influence householder energy consumption behavior changing ? Can the house quality influence the householder electricity energy consumption or useful activities to be more or less. In general, house owners have both intentions for whose property. One intention is living the house by householder himself or herself or householder with families themselves. Another intention is that renting to others to receive rent income (landlord). So, in the housing market, the housing consumer includes either the property owner intents to rent to others to live for rent income aim or the property buyers intents to buy the house to be house owner to live. Does these both different property purchase intentions, which will influence the householder's attitude to use electricity energy consumption desire to be more or less, due to the householder's demand to whose house quality factor influence? This is one interesting question concerns the householder electricity energy consumption desire change to the householder, due to house's investment or house's living intention influences to house quality factor.

How does house quality factor influence to householder electricity energy consumption desire to be more or less? Has it relationship between house quality and house investment or living intention to cause house quality demand to influence the householder electricity energy consumption desire change or demand to be more or less? Has it relationship between regional housing market living or rent investment intentions, housing quality and electricity energy consumption more or less desire? I suppose that the determinants of the residential electricity energy demand form space-heating and cooking, due to the property quality demand influence and the householder's living or rent investment intention influence both, which will influence the householder's electricity energy consumption or useful behavior when he/she/they is/are living in the house.

I argue that rent properties are not only consumer goods, but it also constitute financial market assets. It is therefore reasonable to assume that rational (rent income investment intention) investors choose to raise housing quality (e.g. thermal insulation technological installing at home, heating or cooling technology or artificial intelligent window, lighting, door opening or closing) in order to attract many people choose to rent whose house to live. The householder's aim is to achieve an acceptable return on investment (ROI) or raising rent income aim when he/she rents whose house to anyone, it is easy to attract many people to choose to pay higher rent his/her house to live in the property rent market. Moreover, the another important factor is that rents and future house sale prices of properties differ regionally (or even locally), and largely depend on housing market fundamentals, such as either the house living buyer's income levels or the house rent buyer's income levels, vacancy rates, and/ or householder investor's expectations.

Thus, if the householder expects to rent whose house and raises rent to attract many people choose to rent whose house to live, who will attempt to install many new technology in order to satisfy their high quality of life need when they can pay higher rent to rent to choose to rent whose houses to live. Their aim only achieves to raise housing quality, but any new technology will lead to increase electricity energy consumption or use in the house.

Hence, any high quality of houses will influence the householder to use or consume more electricity energy at home. It means that the householder will choose to consume or use more electricity energy at home, if he/she or the family householder demands to live more comfortable house and he/she/they can have high quality of living life at home. This comfortable living demand to the householder (property renter or property buyer) view point can explain why the better quality of house factor will influence the electricity energy consumption desire to the householder also to be more daily.

I shall indicate one home electricity energy consumption experiment, it indicated that utilizing aggregate data on regional space-heating energy consumption form over 300,000 apartment buildings in 97 German planning regions. The study applies structural equation modelling to estimate the influence of housing market fundamentals on the level of housing quality, and subsequently on regional electricity energy consumption. Consequently, it suggests that housing market fundamental explain regional differences in the housing quality.

In particular, findings show that the level of per capita income, investor' expectations about future housing market development as well as vacancy all explain regional differences in housing quality has a significant impact on electricity energy consumption.

In the way, this experiment can indicate evidence that regional housing market fundamental have a substantial influence on regional levels of housing quality and energy consumption desires to the German regional householders.

This Germany regional householder experiment found important implications for high or low housing quality of the regional property building and householders either property living or property rent intention of comfortable living feeling need factor which will influence the regional property householder electricity energy consumption desire to be raised or reduced. These factors will influence the consequence of electricity energy demand to be increased or decreased needs every day for the regional householder as well as the country's electricity energy supplier(s) can gather the regional properties whether they are high or low quality to predict the regional properties householders' electricity energy consumption supply budget more accurate. It implies that an important determinant of residential housing quality will have possible to influence electricity energy demand to be more or less for long term. IN particular, this Germany regional residential experiment can explain and find an important role in formulating assumptions about the quality factor has chance to influence the regional residential future levels of electricity energy efficiency and consumption in the country. Hence, housing developments and electricity energy firms can follow this regional residential housing quality factor to evaluate whether the regional housing market is the corresponding investment patterns as well as the energy researchers can follow the regional residential housing quality whether it is high or low housing quality factor to evaluate the more accurate models of regional electricity energy demand to any regional residential householders' houses in the country.

In consumer behavioral view point, it explains that if the country government expected many householders feel to need to spend much electricity energy or have much electricity energy useful demand or desire at home. The country government ought to encourage the country residential property or house developers choose to build many houses which have technological product installed to satisfy the regional householders' residential comfortable living need when they choose the regions to build the high quality houses to let them to live. Then, the regional householders will be influenced to consume or use much electricity energy at homes, due to they feel that they are living at high quality and comfortable and high building technological installed apartments in the country's regions. Then, the country's government and electricity energy provider(s) may be raise much electricity energy efficiency and supply and profit , due to the regional residential householders' electricity energy consumption or useful desire need is therefore influenced to be more by the regional high quality of residential houses factor. So, the regional high quality of residential house factor will have relationship to the regional electricity energy consumption and efficiency to the regional householder's houses.

Otherwise, if the country government felt electricity energy is shortage, it ought encourage the property developers build many low quality and low building technological houses to let householders to live themselves or rent to others to live in the country's different regional residential development market. Due to the low quality of properties and low technological installed to properties factor which will influence any these different regional residential householders to choose method to solve shortage of electricity energy challenge to the country.

In conclusion, to apply consumer behavioral economic theory to property development market, if property quality factor can really influence the householder's electricity energy consumption desire to be used more or less at home daily. The country's property developers can apply this factor to predict property consumer individual property buying consumption behaviors more accurate. For example, if the US property developer planned to build low quality and low technological design buildings and lesser comfortable residential houses in the region in US. Then, its residential householder target will be trended the less acceptable of electricity energy consumption property buyers to choose to buy these regional properties to live in the US region because they can only accept to spend less electricity energy to use when they are living in the houses in order to save money daily. SO, the low quality , less comfortable and low technological installed design residential houses will satisfy their living needs. Otherwise, if the US property developer planned to build high quality and high technological installed design buildings and more comfortable residential houses in the region in US. Then, its residential householder target will be trended to the more acceptable of electricity energy consumption property buyers to choose to buy these regional properties to live in the US region because they can accept to spend more electricity energy to use when they are living in the houses in order to improve their living of quality. So, they wont's consider to spend more expenditure to use electricity energy for any technological products are installed in their properties in order to satisfy their comfortable living needs at their homes every day.

Consequently, property developers can attempt to gather marketing research concerns whether how many people who accept to use more electricity energy or use less electricity energy in order to predict they ought build how many high quality or low quality houses number in different regions more accurate in themselves countries or overseas countries property development market.

Environmental impacts of householder greenhouse gas electricity energy consumption activities

Can artificial intelligence influence householders accept to use greenhouse gas electrcity energy in preference? Can environment factor influence householder electricity energy consumption activities? Has environment factor relationship to influence householder electricity energy consumption behaviors? Socially, householder electricity energy consumption provides us with sources of living satisfaction , but if any sudden environment factor changes, whether it will influence householder consume or use more or less electricity energy decision at home. However, I assume householder electricity energy consumption will have a considerable proportion of the environmental impacts be influenced by our way of life and our economic decision of electricity energy consumption behavior.

What different environmental factors will influence householder electricity energy consumption decision? The external environmental factors include, for example, the country's electricity firms or government changes to electricity energy regulations, electricity energy production technologies change and business practices and government policies changing etc. different external environmental factors will influence any country's electricity energy consumption to householders' consumption desire to be more or less. It will also require changes to influence the householders to consume which kinds of electric products which are needed to be used in different electricity energy natural manufacturing resources.

Why does these external environmental factors impact householders' any behaviors to influence them to concern to use more or less electricity energy power or which kinds of electricity energy products choice at homes. How any why environmental factors impact will influence householder activities at home, such as electricity energy consumption and choice? What are the key components of external environmental factors influence householders' electricity energy consumption behaviors. I shall explain as below:

Firstly, we need to know whether what external environments are which can influence why and how householders need to change their activities to choose more or less or which kinds of energy power to be provided to them to use at home. Who is householder? Householder is an individual, family, or group of individuals living together as unit in a home. Consumption of electricity energy at home may be cooking food needs, needing have colder feeling to turn on fan or air condition at home in summer or needing have warm feeling to turn on heater at home in winter, watching television programs or listening music , playing computer games or used computers activities , reading activities and applying artificial intelligent technological tools to help householders to open or close homes' windows, doors etc. different home equipment which need to use electricity energy provisions. SO, their home activities need to turn on lighting electric tools , televisions, music machines, radios etc. different equipment which need to use electricity energy provision at home. SO, the purpose of householder consumption means consumption by individuals living in a household and it includes consumption both in and outside the home. Why does environmental impacts link to householders' electricity energy consumption? I shall focus on discussing of greenhouse gases (GHGS) energy product how any why it can influenced to householders to use.

The environmental impacts will influence this kind of greenhouse gases (GHGS) energy in the product lifecycle or delivery of the service to link the householder's energy consumption at home such as these several aspects:

Extraction and greenhouse gases production (supply number), physical distribution (delivery far long or close near short distance between the greenhouse gases manufacturing factory and the greenhouse gases supplier), resources consumed by marketing and retail activities (

householder's needs to use the quantity of the greenhouse gases energy product), the greenhouse gases consumers search and purchasing activities(e.g. travel to shops, internet purchasing channel, , finding the which kinds of greenhouse gases products from internet, magazines, newspapers, radio advertisements etc. different medias,) , post-use greenhouse gases energy disposal (resale, reused or rubbish). The householder's physical behavioral impact environmental factor will influence how and why he/she chooses to consume greenhouse gases energy daily , e.g. impacts of a housing development, or a wind –farm that supplies greenhouse gases with power. So, the householder's greenhouse gases energy consumption behavior which will depend upon individual personal and subjective perspectives and value.

So, the householder's useful behavior or attitude of greenhouse gases energy product which will influence how he/she/ the family use or consume greenhouse gases energy, such as the householder individual environmental protection attitude which can impact how he/she/the family spends the quantity of greenhouse gases energy every day at home, if the householder does not expect our air or water or land is polluted , due to extraction of any natural gas resources to be manufactured any kinds of greenhouse gases products. Then, this environmental pollution issue will influence some householders choose to reduce to use more quantity of greenhouse gases products every day. Another environmental factors include the bio relates the (unsustainable) use of resources to avoid wasting much greenhouse gases energy to cause greenhouse gases energy supply shortage, avoiding the cause negative impacts of quality life , e.g. noise causing when the extraction of any natural resource from lands to the householder's house is near to the natural resource extraction land and health impacts, e.g. when the greenhouse gas householder user who often use the kind of greenhouse gas product when it is used to cook or heat any equipment to cause they to breathe dirty air at home often. These impacts can be measured in different ways include: monetary costs or loss, physical quantities of resources used or waste or pollution produced and the burden the greenhouse gases energy place on environmental resources. All of these external environment factors will impact the householder individual attitude or behavior how to use or consume greenhouse gases energy product at home.

All these environmental factors concern householder greenhouse gases energy consumer individual consumption attitude is influenced by environment pollution, greenhouse resource supply shortage challenge, greenhouse gases influence the householder's negative quality of life, negative health impacts, noise, waste money , raising economic cost to the householder which will impact whether how the householder choose to use the quantity of greenhouse gases product or the kinds of greenhouse gases products or other kinds of electricity energy products.

However, these are other external environmental factors which can impact how the householder decides to use greenhouse gas product at home. They include: the changes of energy regulation, e.g. the country government has quota number implementation to prohibit to import above the limited quantities of any kinds of greenhouse gas products to any countries. So, when the greenhouse gas energy supplying quantity is decreased, but if the country has may householders who need to buy different kinds of greenhouse gases products to be used at home. Then, the different kinds of import greenhouse gases energy products prices will be raised in possible, due to demand is more than supply in the country's greenhouse gas energy product market. Consequently, if the greenhouse gas energy price us risen above the general social acceptable level to the home greenhouse gas energy product householder consumers. Finally, it will influence them to choose to buy other kinds of gas energy products to replace the greenhouse gas energy product to use at home.

Another side, if the country's greenhouse gas energy manufacturing supplier sudden changes its greenhouse gas energy production technologies to choose to concentrate on manufacturing other kinds of energy products. Then, the greenhouse gas energy supply quantities will be only decreased, even future one day , it will cause greenhouse gas supply shortage challenge to let the country's home greenhouse gas householder consumers who can not buy enough quantity of any kinds of greenhouse gas energy products to satisfy their electricity needs at home every day. Consequently, when future on day , the country greenhouse gas energy manufacturer has none any quantity of greenhouse energy products to supply to the country's greenhouse energy householders to use at home. The, they must only choose other kinds of new energy products to replace the traditional useful greenhouse gas energy products to be used at homes.

In conclusions, these non-controlled external environmental factors can impact and influence the country's every householder consumer individual attitude or consumption behavioral change to how any why the country's householders either choose to buy much or less quantity of greenhouse gas products to use at home.

The effect of house space occupancy
and building characteristics on
householder electricity energy use

In general, society believes large space size occupancy house building characteristics factor which will influence householder use more energy at home, e.g. in summer, when the householder is living at the large space size occupancy house, who ought turn on all air conditions or fans at sleeping rooms or eating room or studying room. So, if the householder's house has two to three or more sleeping rooms. Then, he / she needs to buy more air conditions or fans in order to let all rooms' temperature to be fallen down to let he /she feel more cool comfortable feeling when the temperature is above 30 degree or more extreme hot in summer weather. Otherwise, when the temperature is low, e.g. between 0 degree to 10 degree or below 0 degree in winter weather. When the householder is living in one large space size occupancy appartment, which has thee to five sleeping rooms , even more and two studying rooms and one eating room, even more as well as every room has one heater. Then, he / she must turn on all heaters to let who to feel warm feeling when he / she is staying in the house. It brings these interesting questions.

Will large or small size space occupancy housing characteristics influence any householder often turn on heater or air condition or fan in whole house space occupancy area in order to the householder feels warmer or cooler feeling when he /she is staying in the house?

Has any space occupancy housing characteristics relationship to influence any householder to turn on heater or air condition or fan in whole house space occupancy area in order to the householder feels warmer or cooler feeling when he /she is staying in the house?

Does it bring positive relationship between turning on long time fan or air condition or heater and the house occupancy space characteristics is large or small size?

I shall attempt to give psychological evidences to explain the householder's house space occupancy area large or small size factor whether it can influence the householder choose to do long time or short time turning on heater or air condition or fan behavior in order to let he/she/the family to feel more cooler or warmer comfortable feeling when he/she/the family is staying in the house in summer or winter weather.

Does the house occupancy space size characteristics factor is the only one or important factor to influence the householder choose to turn on long or short time fan or air condition or heater in the house to let him/her/ the family to feel more cooler or warmer comfortable feeling in summer or winter weather?

I feel that it is not exact right , due to the householder's house space occupancy size whether it is large or small characteristics to influence the householder choose to turn on long time or short time fan or air condition or heater time to let him /her/ the family to feel more cooler or warmer when he / she / the family is staying at home in summer or winter weather. The reason is because that the lifestyle of living quality need is different between developed countries and developing countries. The lifestyle of living quality factor will change the country's householder's expectation about the quality of living life. For example, for Africa, Korea, China , Japan, Hong Kong etc. developing countries. On the lifestyle of living quality need to these developing countries' householders aspect, that will cause a high environmental burden when they need to often turn on air conditions to satisfy more cooler feeling when they are staying at homes in summer or they need often to turn on heaters to satisfy more warmer feeling when they are staying at home in winter. Due to if their houses are large size space occupancy characteristics and they have more than at least two sleeping rooms and studying rooms and eating rooms and toilets number. Then, these householders who are developing countries' large space occupancy size characteristics houses, they won't like often turn on heaters long time to keep more warmer in their indoor whole space area in winter or they won't like often turn on air conditions or fans long time to keep more cooler in the their indoor whole space area house environment in summer .

The reason is possible because that the developing countries' householder chooses often to turn on their heaters or air conditions or fans long time in their houses when they are staying long time in their houses and their houses space occupancy sizes are very large, it will bring the electricity energy to be used more to these developing countries' householders' large space occupancy size characteristic houses. It means that the electricity fee will be also increased due to they often turn on heaters or air conditions or fans long time to keep their indoor temperature to be more cooler in summer or more warmer in winter. So, it seems that the developing countries' householders are living in the house whose space occupancy have very large size characteristics and more than two rooms house characteristics in the developing countries as above. Then, they won't often choose to turn on heaters or air conditions or fans long time to keep more cooler or warmer feeling in their house whole indoor space occupancy environment when they are often staying at home long time.

Their lifestyle of living comfortable feeling are lesser than the developed countries householders. Consequently, their lesser cooling or warming comfortable demand of living lifestyle factor will change their attitudes to use air conditions or fans or heaters turning on time in order to limit heaters or air conditions or fans turning on time to be shorter than the developed countries houeholders' heaters or air conditions or fans turning on time at homes. Due to the long time turnong on air conditions, fans , heaters at the developing countries' householders' homes, it will cause to spend much electricity energy to lead electricity fee charges to be raised to the developing countries' householders ' homes when they are often staying at homes in summer or winter weather. Hence, the house space occupancy large size characteristics ought not influence the developing countries householders choose to turn on air conditions , fans or heaters long time in order to let them to feel more cooler or warmer at homes in summer or winter weather.

So, the developing countries' house space occupancy large size characteristics householders won't be more acceptable to pay higher electricity energy fee when they are staying at homes at summer or winter weather. Due to they do not often choose to turn on heaters, air conditions or fans long time during they are staying at homes. Otherwise, the developed countries, e.g. UK, UK , France, Germany, Swiss, Singapore, Italy etc. countries. In general, these developed countries' householders' living lifestyle quality needs are higher than the developing countries. So, when the summer or winter weather is coming, if the temperature is extreme cold, e.g. below than 0 degree or it is extreme hot, e.g. higher than 30 degee. Then these developed countries' householders will easy accept to turn on air conditions or fans or heaters long time at home in order to keep their appartment in door temperature to be more cooler in extreme hot in door environment or more warmer in extreme cold in door environment when these develoculd countries' householders are often staying at homes long time at night after their day time working time or schooling time. Because these developed counties' householders' quality of living lifestyle needs or demands are higher than the developing countries' householders. So, they won't consider that they will pay more electricity fee , due to they often turn on air conditions, fans or heaters long time to let them to feel more comfortable in cooler or warmer indoor large size space occupancy environment. So, it seems that the electricity energy efficiency will be raised to the developed countries' householders who are living in the house space occupancy large size characteristics and they will be possible to pay more electricity fees during they are often staying at home in extreme hot summer or extreme cold winter weather.

In conclusion, due to the living lifestyle quality need (demand) is different between the developed countries' householders and the developing countries' householders. It will influence the householders' long time or short time spending time on air conditions or fans or heaters indoor space occupancy size characteristics environment in order to achieve more cooler or more warmer feeling in their houses. Consequently, the long or short time of turning on air conditions, fans, heaters for the developed or developing countries householders' activities factor will be more influential to compare the house space occupancy large or small size characteristics factor to influence their cooler or warmer feeling in their houses. SO, the house indoor environment electricity energy consumption efficiency degree to the developing or developed countries' every householder house in summer or winter to the developing or developed householders in summer or winter weather , which is more influenced by the living lifestyle qualty factor to the either developed countries or developing countries householders. Hence, any developed or developing countries' electricity suppliers need to consider the building areas of property development market buyers their living style quality demands (needs) whether their living style quality demands are higher or lesser than the other building areas of property development market, they ought not consider whether the building locations of the houses' space occupation sizes whether they are large or small sizes in order to evaluate the householders will live at the building areas of property development locations ,whose electricty energy spending efficiency more accurate.

How to help low income houehold earners to reduce not essential electricity energy expenditure spending at homes

Has it relationship between the householder income and the electricity energy needs? How to evaluate the subsidies and social tariffs to assist lower income earners to analyze household energy consumption more accurate?

Electricity energy is essential needs for every householder at home, e.g. lighting, cooking power, healthcare, sanitation, cooler or warmer temperature indoor control at home. However, for lower income household earners, it its burden when they need often to use electricity energy to supply power to any home electricity tools to do any acticities at homes. If any these countries' lower income householder earner target can not get the reasonable subsidies to assist them to solve any electricity energy tools' electricity energy poer needs. Due to their lower income leve, it is possible that to knfluence them have enough electricity supply to help them to use to cook rice and food and vegatabe to eat, boil water to drink, turning on light tools to help them to read, watch TV, listen radio, music any entertainment or essential needs at homes at night or morning afternoon time. These lower income household earners will be easy to sick , due to they have no enough electricity supply to help them to use use electric bottles to boil water or cook food to eat. Then they only drink not boiled water or not cooked food to eat at homes in possible, due to they have no enough income to pay electricity fees every month.

Hence, how to evaluate the lower income household earners' electricity fee need (demand) level in order to provide the reasonable subsidies amount to assist every country's low income household earner to help them to pay the reasonable electricity fee which is one important issue to every country's government today. It brings this question: How to evaluate or analyze or predict every lower income household individual or family earner's every month electricity energy demand (need) more accurate?

It is one essential issue to be value to consider to every country's government. Moreover, to the estent that energy subsidies must be essential to be provided by public sources to all low income household earners or that a social tariff may be designed for improving access to energy for certain low income social earner groups. Hence, how to structure the energy subsidies between energy and income levels to be better target, such public mechanisms, and to avoid regressive subsidies unfairly. For example, India and China these both countries ' income poverty and energy poverty population are the large number. So , these both countries' governments need to focuse on more aggregated effects and analyze the effects of rural electrification at the local level on the decrease in energy poverty in rural low income poverty and energy poverty householders. Therefore, every country government needs to point regressivity of the subsidy for electricity. There is room to analyze to what extent low income household earners along the income distribution demand some forms of energy, and to suggest better and fair low income targeting household earners energy subsidies supply policies.

Each government does not only consider energy issues from a social point of view, it also needs have a manner to consider a possible link between energy, hunger reduction, and food security for each country's low income household earners group. So, every government has responsibility to calculate the determinants of different sources of energy consumption at the low income houehold earner level for urban and rural both populations in order to evaluate the electricity subsidies and to test whether every low income householder earner characteristics plays a role in determining energy consumption.

In general, in the use of energy measured as that for cooking, such as LPG reduces the exposure of households to hazardous, increases the consumption of different types of foods and medicines, improves the distribution of time between household memners, enables studys with more light, reduces the use of digital computer entertainment tools at home, and moderates the use of wood as fuel, preventing deforestation. These methods are the best suggestions to help low income householder earner groups to reduce time to use electricity at homes. When they spend less time to use electricity to do any not essential activities, e.g. watching television, playing electric games from home computers, listening music. They only use electricity to turn on light read, to turn on rice cooker to cook, when they feel hungey to eat. Then, I believe that these social low income household earner groups will reduce to pay much not essential electricity energy expenditure at homes. Hence, every country government ought need to persuade low income household earners to avoid to use electricity to do any not essential activities in order to raise electricity energy consumption in long term time.

It will bring less amount of energy subsidies expenditure benefits to every country's government. Hence, the success to persuade any countries' low income household earners to reduce to spend much time to do any electric entertainment activities of consumption behaviors at homes often. This is the most efficient and the most successful energy subsidiary method to help them to reduce electricity energy expenditure when they are staying at homes. Hence, if any country government expected the low income household earners can continue really reduce electricity energy expenditure, they need to learn to do the meaning essential activities which are needed to use electricity at home habitally. Then, they can change their electricity useful entertainment living habit, e.g. using computers to play games, listening music, watching television entertainment habits at homes to cause essential daily needs of electricity useful living habit, e.f. using cookers to cook rice or cook food to eat, turning on lights to read , turning on heaters to bath, turning on air conditions to keep cool temperature or turning on heaters to keep warm temperature at homes. Consequently, they won't need to pay much electricity expenditure at home, due to their waste useful electricity entetainment living habits have changed to do any essential useful electricity activities at homes.

Another kind of method to reduce the determinants of energy demand to the low income householder earners. The governments can persuade them to consider the variation factor can influence their electricity energy expenditure are increased or decreased at homes. It is not the electricity or gas price is increased from the electricity suppliers. It is that their bad living habits of waste electricity or gas to do any not essential activities at homes. e.g. the householder often turn on light tools to read or listen music or watch television in whole night, he/she ought need to sleep at night, but he/she does not go to bed to sleep in whole night. He/she chooses to turn on light to do these activities. Then, he/she will waste much electricity at whole night. Also, some householders like to bath more than half hour, even one hour, when it is winter, they need to turn on heaters to provide electricity to cause the bath room has warm water to provide to them to bath, Their long time bathing behaviors will be also waste electricity or gas energy from long time heating in bath rooms. So, they need to change their waste electricity consumption living behaviors at homes.

So, I suggest that some low income household earners will need to be taught to change their bad using electricity enery living habits from governments' public relation promotion in order to change the low income household earners' bad or incorrected useful electricity or gas living attitude to achieve and to avoid them often to do electricity or gas energy waste behaviors at homes. So, different countries' governments need to teach them how to do the correct or right electricty or gas useful activities (living habits) or let them know or feel how to use their electricity or gas which can help them to reduce to waste the not essential extra electricity or gas energy. Consequently, they must reduce electricity or gas expenditure as well as electricity or gas shortage challenge won't be caused by their electricity or gas useful waste behaviors (activities) at homes.

In conclusion, energy subsidies method is not the best solution to help low income household earners to reduce to use electricity or gas energy. Because it is only short term benefit to reduce their electricity or gas expenditure at homes. The best solution is that to let them to know or feel why and how they have responsibilities to change their incorrent or wrong electricity or gas consumption bad habits in order to avoid global electricity or gas energy is waste to be used, even it is caused shortage from householders' energy waste behaviors.

Factors influence householder energy
efficient consumption behaviors
at homes

What factors can influence householders how to use energy in efficient way at homes. It depends on different countries householders' living habits to cause their choices to use energy efficiently at homes. In general, global householders energy every day consumption or use aims include cooking, heating, and cooling or warming rooms, lighting , water-boiled use and computer playing games entertainment etc. activities at homes every day. Some activities are often essential at homes, e.g. cooking, cooling or warming temperature in rooms, lighting , water-boiled use. So, their activities must not avoid to use energy at homes often. Otherwise, some activities are not essential at homes, e.g. playing entertainment games from computers, cooling rooms in summer, listening music, watching television etc. these activities. The householder can choose either to use energy to turn on these equipment tools or not to do these non essential activities at homes often. In general, householders rely on energy to make ourselves lives comfortable, productive and enjoyable. However, global householders need to learn how we can use energy resources wisely because global every householder has responsibility to manage resources includes: reducing total energy use and using energy more efficiently in order to avoid energy shortage crise occurrence. The choices are make about how we use energy, e.g. turning machines off when not in use of choosing to buy energy efficieny appliances will have increasing impacts on the quality of our environment and lives.

Energy conservation includes any behavior that results in the use of less energy. Energy efficiency involves the use of technology that requires less energy to perform the same function. For example, a compact fluorescent light buld that uses less energy to produce the same amount of light as an incandescent light buib is an example of energy efficiency. So, a householder's decision to place an incanadescent light bulb with compact fluorescent is an example of energy conservation. So, as individuals, every countries' householder choices and actions can result in a significant reduction in the amount of energy used in each sector of the economy.

So, I bring this interesting question: What factors can influence householder to choose to do any efficient energy consumption or useful behaviors at homes? I believe every countries' householders will have their different living attitudes and their living attitudes can influence their behaviors or activities to choose hoe to use energy at home. I shall indicate some countries' householders' living attitudes to explain the factors can influence them to use energy efficiency at homes as below:

● Is the low income and rising price of modern fuels both factors best to influence Nigeria householders choose to use energy efficiently?

Firstly, for Nigeria householders energy consumption habit at homes example, it is richly with natural resources, modern energy resources which provide many householders with biomass (mostly firewood) and some other householders modern energy sources, such as kevosene, liquefied, petroleum, gas and electricity for their use. So, it is one country which can manufacture to provide energy for itself to use. It doesn't need to depend on other countries to import any kinds of energy to householders to buy to use at homes. But, it has social challenge, the poverty problem in Nigeria goes beyond low income, savings and growth rate, due to its low level of education, poor governamce, high level of unemployment factors influence. It is important to know how Nigeria householders meet their basic energy needs between poverty and energy can bde described in terms of quality and quantity of energy used. Generally, most poor householders use biomass fuels because of affordability and they (householders) do not have energy equipment (such as, gas cookers, electric cookers etc.) . So, it seems Nigeria householders won't demand their living quality to be improved. It implies that they will use any kinds of energy efficiently at homes, e.g. gas, electricity, due to they find themselves in energy poverty. Although, this country has enough nature resources to manufacture energy to provide to householders to use, but due to many people are low income group, so they won't spend too much expenditure to buy much energy to use at homes. So, the rising prices of modern fuels, such as liquefied, petroleum , gas (LPG) and electricity and their erratic supply have made many householders revert to the use of traditional fuel, such as firewood and charcoal.

It brings this questions: Is the low income and rising price of modern fuels both factors best to influence Nigeria householders choose to use energy efficiently?

The hypothes is predicated on the economic theory of consumer behavior. However, when income increases, householders not only consume more of the same goods, they also need higher quality . So, it applies economic theory to householder's energy consumption behavior at home. It explains why low living standards induce greater dependence on firewood and other biomass fuels owing to a combination of income and substitution effects, such as Nigeria low income household energy home users case. it explains why Nigeria householders can accept to use firewood and charaval traditional energy to replace liquefied, petroleum , gas (LPG) and electricity modern energy . So, economic theory explains the Nigeria household energy users why they can accept to use traditional energy to replace modern energy and their energy useful or consumption behaviors are efficient at homes. Although, Nigeria has enough natural resource to manufacture modern energy to supply to householders to use at homes. But, due to these modern energy products prices are raised to the price level of householders who can not accept. it causes to Nigeria householders only choose to buy the cheap biomass, firewoods to replace high price of modern energy products to use at home often. So, they can accept their quality of living to be fallen down. So, expensive modern energy product price is one factor to influence some countries' householders to choose to buy cheap traditional poor quality of nature energy, e.g. firewood or biomass, to use at homes. Hence, they can raise energy efficiency to use when they choose to use traditional nature energy to replace modern nature energy at homes.

● Does season factor influence New Zealand householders' energy consumption behaviors at homes

Secondly, for New Zealand householders energy consumption habits at homes , for example, their living quality needs are general comfortable need feeling. Their countries' houses of space heating was found to average 34% of total housholder energy use. The relation to space heating includes low indirect temperature are associated with persistent under-heating , whether some space heating sources tend to be higher or lower in winter indoor temperature than others and winter indoor temperatures are compared to international benchmarks and established healthy temperature ranges. So, New Zealand occupant's perceptions of winter indoor temperature conditions are presented and explored in relation to heating patterns and household energy consumption. So, it seems that NZ winter temperature is low. Moreover, it will influence householders need to turn on heaters to keep more warmer feeling indoor. Then, they will use more electricity energy. In special, if the householders' houses spaces are large sizes . Hence, their heaters need long time to keep whole houses' areas or spaces or rooms temperature to be rised up in order to let they do not feel very cold in winter. So, NZ's winter extreme cold weather will influence householders' energy use or consumption to be increased in winter.

The electricity efficiency to every NZ householder is very high in winter to compare spring, summer, autumn seasons. Hence, if NZ electricity suppliers expected to forecast electricity consumption more accurate in NZ. In order to ease the life for both electric net designers and electricity suppliers, it was decided to find out, how the NZ weather conditions and every householder's house space size factors to influence the power consumption to NZ householders. If there is a clear trend observed , then this relation can be used for power consumption forecasts to NZ householders.

Why does NZ weather condition factor and householder's house space size factor can predict householders' electricity consumption at homes. Due to geographic location on the global the lowest south sets specific conditions for weather, such as NZ's south island geographic location is near to south ocean in our earth. It is a country where average annual temperatures are well between 10 degree to below 10 degree at NZ south island special geographic location to near to the sourth ocean in our earth at the same time.

However, large part of mankind is living in the conditions where there are four different seasons in NZ geographic location, dark winter, which is cold and snowy, spring with rising temperature and high precipitation, sunny , dry and rather hot summer, and windy and wet autumn. These conditions lead to different patterns in electric appliances use in NZ householders, in special, in NZ south island householders. If trends in electric energy use have substantial correlation with weather conditions, this can help NZ electric energy suppliers and producers to forecast electricity consumption and thus organize and manage production of electric energy.

Consequently, it will lead to much more stability in energy supply to NZ every householder. For example, when the NZ energy supplier gathers data concerns every householder's house space size data, e.g. the house has how many sleeping rooms, toilets, bath rooms, eating rooms and reading rooms number, even the house has how many family members are living in every NZ geographical location. Then if it can follow different location of NZ houses spaces sizes whether they are large or small space size as well as whethe every house has how many family members are living to evaluate whether how much electricity efficiency can satisfy their comfortable living needs in winter. Then, it can evaluate whether they will use how much electricity efficiency for their needs in different seasons. If in winter, many householders are living in the large space size house in the geographic location. Then, it is possible that the geographic location is householders will use much electricity efficiency and where geographic location hosueholders who will be possible to pay the most highest electricity fee to compare the other geographic location of small space size of house householders. Hence, weather factor is the most influential to change NZ householders ' electricity energy consumption behaviors at homes.

● Urbanization level and income per capita both tangible factors as well as temperature (weather variation factor) will have close relationship to influence China householder energy consumption or useful needs at home every day

For China householder energy consumption habit example, what factors can determine to impact this country's householders energy useful behavior at homes? Can the impacts of these factors be quntified? What are China householder energy consumption trends and characteristics? I shall explan as below:

I believe the influential factors include these three aspects to China householder energy users: Income per capita, urbanization level an annual average temperature (weather). These factors will influence any China householder energy useful or consumption behavior at homes.

Temperature (weather variation factor) is intangible from eastern region to western region of Chin, variances largely depend upon economic level and the provincial level. So, some regions were warmer and cooler temperature will influence the regional China householder how to use electricity. In addition, th influence of urbanization level varies according to income level as well as the urbanization level has more significant impact on the structure and efficiency of China householder energy consumption thatn on its quantity. So, the urbanization level and income per capita both tangible factors will have close relationship to influence China householder energy consumption or useful needs at home every day. Moreover, these two tangible factors (urbanization level and income per capita both factors) have the more influential to impact China any one of household family energy consumption or useful habit to compare temperature factor at home. Because temperature can only influence than to choose to turn on heaters to keep more cooler in summer or turn on air conditions (fans) to keep more warmer in winter.

The electricity energy needs for these equopment tools which will be influenced less. Otherwise, the urbanization level and income per family householder how to choose to spend more or less electricity or gas etc. energy at homes. Because in behavioral economy view point, when individual householder has more income and the urban in the China geographic location is lising many high income and high household families memebrs to every house. Then, the urbanization household energy household enery useful or consumption level will be raised. Such as China household electricity users case, e.g. large cities have many high income and many houses have more than four families members to live on one house together. Then, the electricity or gas energy efficiency will be influenced to rise. The city urbanization and per capita income level is high to these large cities have high to income population, who are living in these cities in China.

Moreover, the impact of lifestyle on energy use mainly reflects types and purposes of fuels are chosen by different China households factor which will influence the urbanization level of energy choice use. China is a country with typical binary economics and social diversity and these is significant difference in the consumption pattern between urban and rural regions. Urban residents consume high-quality energy, such as electricity, natural gas , heating power, solar energy and gasoline. For rural residents, usually use coal, and bismass energy because they are cheaper price energy products which requires much time and labor and are heavy indoor pollutants . The difference in energy consumption pattern between urban and rural China residents is closely related related to living of quality needs, building structure, e.g. steel or stone etc. different materials, manufacture, easily access clean and effective feels through the electric grid, natural gas network and district heating systems.

Therefore, it explains why urbanization level is as an integrated variable reflecting social progress situation to influence urban and rural regions, such as large cities , small cities and rural countryside regions' household energy consumption or useful behaviors which have differnet kinds of fuel useful demands and energy efficiencies qualify and quantity demand, or needs at homes. Consequently, it explains, urbanization level and income per captia level both factors are more influential to China household energy consumption at home to compare temperature (weather , seasonal) factor.

● Employment rates or gross domestic product macro economic variation factor, residential space size factor, and the government's implementation of energy labeling schemes provide significant impacts on Taiwan residential electricity consumption .

For Taiwan householder electricity consumption characteristics in the residential sector, which has different factors and pattern to compare China householder electricity householder electricity consumption habit at home. Although, they are the same Asia country. I shall explain these reasons as below:

For Taiwan electricity householder factors influence their energy useful or consumption behaviors at homes. The main factors can influence their electricity energy useful patterns include: employment rates or gross domestic product macro economic variation factor, residential space size factor, and the government's implementation of energy labeling schemes provide significant impacts on Taiwan residential electricity consumption . However, the impacts of electricity raising price and the energy supply reducing shortage efficiency standards do not significant to influence the Taiwan residential electricity consumption behavior at sources.

It means that it won't influence Taiwan householders to use electricity or gas or any kinds of energy number to be reduced, even the Taiwan government energy suppliers sudden raise, any kinds of energy price and reduce to supply energy to satisfy Taiwan householders daily essential needs at homes.

In fact, Taiwan had improved gross domestic product (GDP) and it had raised employment rates recently. So, many Taiwanese has jobs to work, due to Taiwan economy had improved to be better. So, growth had also raised. The economy improvement causes many Taiwanese had enough jobs to work, due to new businesses are set up. Many consumers excit any kinds of businesses are invested to Taiwan from overseas or local investors. So, consumption is grown, the electricity consuming applicances are selected, as the household consumer focus grousp number if also influenced to be increased. So, Taiwan economy had improved to be better, it will encourage many electricity consuming applicances products are encouraged to excited to be selected to seel in Taiwan. Due to many different kinds of electricity consuming appliances are supplied to attract Taiwanese to choose to buy to bring to their homes for cooking, boiling water, or keeping rooms to be cooler or warmer temperature confortable feeling intention in winter or summer seasons. So, these electricity consuming appliances, e.g. rice cookers, heaters, air conditions, fans, bathing gas heaters etc. different home electricity consuming appliances will be increased to supply to satisfy Taiwan householders' needs. When they decide to buy any news electricity consuming applicances to bring to homes to use.

● Environment scientists' education message how to influence Greece householders home energy consumption behaviors from primary energy to change secondary energy

Finally , I shall indicate Greece, this western which will influence this country's householders have desires to do household energy conservation patterns or conservation energy consumption behaviors or energy conservation activities at homes. I shall explain the social economic variable, such as consumers' income and family size variation factor which can influence the different Greece family household members differences towards energy conservation preferences. IN addition, the variable, such as environmental information feedback and consciousness of energy problems are characteristics of the energy saver consumer.

Why and how can environmental pollution , environmental protection, energy conservation information message can influence Greece householders to choose to do energy use consumption conservation or less energy useful behaviors at homes. It is one interesting energy efficient use behaviors , due to Greece householders are influenced by energy conservation or environmental protection message.

In fact, scientists agree overconsumption of natural resources is a major threat to oue lives in earth. Environmental problems like greenhouse effect, ozone layer depletion, and acid rain effect are not any more problems of a specific region or environmental problem. Also, economic theory is indicated that in order to gain comfort and time households are becoming excessive energy users, neglecting the environmental impact of their choices.

Environment scientists bring these environment pollution message to influence Greeks (Greece householders) to change their energy consumption behaviors at homes. The environment scientists' message indicate that we are facing global warmth and natural resource and energy shortage challenges. Due to our Earth have limited natural resource numbers to supply to us to manufacture energy, but global population has been increasing every year. Thus, it is possible that we have energy shortage crisis. Also, manufactures are spending too much energy to waste to manufacture any products, the energy will cause air or water pollution in manufacturing process or drivers are driving their vehicles to pollute air on the roads.

Hence, environment scientists' message influence Greece householders began to consider these questions concern to reduce fossil fuel energy. Why do we need to Safety in using fuel and handle gas leaks? Why do we feel town gas smell? How is electricity located at electric station far away from town area? How to solve problems caused by the use of fossil fuels? How to reduce the use of fossil fuels?

Greece householders consider to solve the problems, the best way is to reduce thir used of fossil fuel. This helps prevent fossil fuels form being used up too quickly. Also, it helps them to reduce environmental problems because fewer pollutants are given out when less fossil fuels are used. Can human help to reduce the use of fossil fuels? Fossil fuels are mainly in power station. Although they use some fossil fuels for our gas cooker and car, it won't make much difference if I use less. Fossil fuel is not used renew primary energy. Most of energy Greece householders use come from fossil fuels, for example, the electricity we use is generated in power stations by burning fossil fuels. The buses they ride use diesel oil. Therefore, they can help reduce the use of fossil fuels by saving energy in Greece daily lives.

The actions that Greece householders can take such as: setting the air-conditioner to a higher temperature, walking instead of using lift, taking a short shower instead of a bath. This reduces the use of the hot water and thus the energy needed to heat the water. Thus, many people can help a lot to reduce our use of fossil fuels to avoid fossil fuel shortage risk occurrence.

Greeks (Greece householders) had been beginning to conern that they will face energy shortage challenge if they can not adopt more energy conservation actions. Because the Greece government began to bring negative environmental pollution and energy shortage challenge message if they often waste to use any kinds of energy, e.g. electricity , gas excessive number efficiency at homes. Then, they will be possible to fac energy shortage and environmental pollution challenge to their country in future one day. So, this energy shortage and environment pollution message has bring predictive negative worries to influence many Greece householder energy home users choose to reduce to avoid the waste of any kinds of energy use at homes.

So, their reducing energy use actions that had encouraged them to cause habits to avoid to waste excess energy to do any non essential electric appliances useful or consumption activities at homes often. Moreover, the environment protection and energy conservation message has changed many Greece householder to make decision and activities to change their lifestyle to b low living quality from high living quality. So, the environment protection and energy conservation message factor has much influential to change Greece household energy users' daily energy conservation or less energy use consumption activities at homes.

Greeks feel greenhouse energy can be environmental protection enegy. A greenhouse can trap heat in the sunlight and keeps the air inside the greenhouse warm enough for plants to grow. The glass roof and walls of a greenhouse let in sunlight but prevent heat from escape, this makes the greenhouse warm inside. Similarly, some gases in the Earth's atmosphere can trap heat from the sun and keep the Earth warm. This is called the greenhouse effect. The gases energy that can trap heat from the sun are called greenhouse gases. It is future one kind of potential primary energy to reduce environmental pollution new energy products for human consuming. So, environmental protection message influence them to consume greenhouse enegy at homes.

So, environment scientists' environment pollution message had influence Greece householders concern to apply seconday energy (environment protection) to replace electricity energy to use at home. They will change energy to use at home. The scientists' messages have more influential Greece householders energy change consumption behaviors at homes. The messages are as below:

There are different forms of energy, e.g. light, heat, sound, wind, water, electrical kinetic, chemical and potential energy. Some form energy is primary energy and it can not renew to use, e.g. light, sound, wind, water, fossil fuel etc. Some form energy is secondary energy and it can renew to use in possible, e.g. nuclear, electric charge battery etc. Why does human need to concern how to manufacture secondary energy? Because it is possible that our natural resource will be consumed all, thus we will face primary energy shortage risk. If human can invent any new form of man-made secondary energy to renew to use in order to avoid primary energy shortage to supply to use to use, then human won't only depend on our Earth natural resource energy supply numbers. We can invent any new secondary energy to renew to use again either replaces primary energy or instead of primary energy limit number supply.

What is energy change? For television energy change power case. Firstly, electrical energy changes to television power to be used by television itself, then it changes to light power, next it changes to light power. How to choose fuel form to use? Due to energy can change to different form of powers to supply different form of power advantages to supply to human to use, so it is possible that we can also invent any secondary man made renew used energy to change different form powers to supply us to use, e.g. nuclear energy changes to light or sound or heat form of powers ; electrical charge batteries changes to light or sound or heat form powers to satisfy our daily life needs.

The environment scientists' energy consumption education influence Greece householders concern how to change to use secondary energy to replace primary energy at homes as below:

For primary natural resource fuel energy example, different fuel has different feature, e.g. easy to burn, safe to use, gives out a lot of energy, inexpensive, produces little air pollution, easy to transport and store. How can we use in different channels, such as heating food, hot pat, driving vehicles.

For example, although coal is not expensive to cause electricity energy for past transportation tool, e.g. traditional coal energy train or our daily home cooking, but it has negative influence to environment air pollution. Hence, we ought to follow the primary natural resource energy's feature to decide how to apply what aspects of our life needs.

For example, if the country's people hope to reduce pollution when who use any kind of energy, e.g. US , Europe energy markets. The energy entrepreneur ought concentrate on manufacturing the kind of energy which can reduce environment pollution to be the least level to supply the country people to use, e.g. electric charge battery supplies to these countries' drivers to drive their vehicles on the roads, wind energy or water energy to manufacture electricity power supply to reduce air or water pollution ; or if the country people hope to buy the inexpensive energy to use, even the energy's quality and performance is worse, e.g. China, India, Hong Kong markets. The energy entrepreneur ought concentrate on manufacturing the lowest cost and enough supply of natural resource to manufacture the kind of energy to sell cheap price to these countries to use, e.g. China, Africa can accept to use e.g. gas, coal, fuel energy to use to compare developed countries people, e.g. UK, US; or if the countries people who hope to use energy which can easy to transport and store, e.g. light coal. The energy entrepreneur can choose to concentrate on manufacturing much coal to supply to the countries people to use, e.g. China, Arica Thus, to choose to manufacture which kinds of energy supply to the countries market people to use, the energy entrepreneur how decides to manufacture which kind of energy, it depends on which kinds of fuel advantages of the countries people most concerning.

What is energy meaning? It is defined a dynamic quality, it is a fundamental entity of nature that is transferred between parts of a system in the production of physical change within the system, and it is usually regarded as the capacity for doing work, and it is usable power (such as heat or electricity) or the resources for producing such power.

Why does secondary energy own investment worth? Because the different forms of primary natural resource energy will have supply shortage crisis, such as natural resources coal, gas, solar, wind, water, geothermal, biomass(organic material) etc. However, human can attempt to explore any undiscovered Earth or Space resource to manufacture any kinds of secondary energies, e.g. nuclear energy, electric recharge battery energy to supply to electric vehicle or space robots transportation tools to use or satisfy our daily life needs in future one day. So any kind of undiscovered secondary man-made renewed used energy resources have potential commercial worth to any energy entrepreneurs, it is possible that they can replace traditional primary energy to supply to human to use for our different aspects of life needs. In the future, the secondary energy demand will increase, when primary energy supply number has decreased form natural exploration. So, it will cause the effect of any demand of secondary energy product to be raised and prices to be increased in possible. Due to global population has been growing up, considerably China and India both countries populations have been increasing rapidly. Scientists predict there are more than 1.2 billion people worldwide will lack access to electricity, and more than 2.5 billion still use wood, charcoal to cook and heat in the future when primary energy has no enough number to supply to us to use. Hence, the fact that demand is this much greater than supply to make energy a prime market for further growth.

Although, secondary energy will have much investment worth, but energy like all other investments will carry risks. The internal and external risk factors include such as: policy is always changing to prohibit which do energy trading more easily between the energy exporting and importing countries, the secondary energy manufacturer itself own abilities to invent and to manufacture any kinds of secondary energy, improved technology can quickly make an technology obsolete, geopolitical rifts can happen overnight, the country's energy consumer (user)'s preferable choice to use which either kinds of secondary energy or secondary energy. So, it seems that (man-made) renewed used secondary energy industry can provide above-average returns, but it can also bring high risk commercial investment.

Traditionally, energy supply companies will apply those methods to operate energy providing businesses. For Shell,. Exxon examples, which had own gas stations, explore and drill for gas on their own. Other companies specialize in a part of the energy market, e.g. leasing oil rigs for example, or operating a pipeline. Energy supplying companies can choose to manufacture any kinds of energy to supply, e.g. trade oil, gas, coal, uranium, electricity etc. Any energy price and supply is demanded on the countries energy users' which kinds of energy most choice need or certain energy commodities to be chose to use popularly. For example, if US most people prefer to use secondary man-made renew used energy more than primary energy. Then, US energy manufacturers ought concentrate on manufacturing much different kinds of secondary man-made renew used energy to prepare to supply to its domestic US market in order to raise secondary energy price to sell in its country. So, the energy manufacturer's energy manufacturing choice, it is depend on which the country's people prefer to use which kinds of energy for their daily life needs.

However, scientists predict secondary energy market will have large market share, due to primary energy will have shortage to explore to supply in our earth and future energy consumers(users) prefer to choose to use more efficiency, less energy consumption, none environment pollution cause, cost effectiveness, renew to use of any kinds of energy. For example, the electricity recharge battery secondary man-made renew used energy is one kind of reducing air pollution power to push any electric battery vehicles to be driven to compare gas energy during drivers are driving their cars on the roads. They can reduce noise and air pollution and drivers can drive safely, who only need to buy one electric recharge battery to recharge in any electric recharge battery stations on streets when the electric recharge battery has no enough power to push their cars and they need to recharge their electric recharge battery drive when they had driven between one to two days. Due to primary energy, e.g. fuel , gas, the kinds of primary energies will have shortage to supply to global drivers to drive their traditional cars. Thus, the electric recharge battery or any undiscovered secondary energy will be future driving market needs. So, man-made renew used secondary energy, e.g. biofuel, hydro-electric, nuclear, will be one kind of efficient, clean, less pollution cause, cost-effective of energy to supply to our global vehicle market, even any other undiscovered new markets. Supposing they are popular to be used for electric vehicle market globally in future one day, then their prices will be decreased and constructed to average car requires up to 1,700 gallons of oil. Also supposing that making average computer requires more than ten times or weight to fossil fuels, every calories of food eaten in the US requires roughly then calories of fossil fuels. Hence, cheap energy will be one successful factor to influence future potential energy consumer (user) individual choice needs. Conversely, ion good economic times, people are more willing to travel, to buy products, and all of which success demand and low process for energy.

In the future, secondary energy will be the best choice to food production market. The modern food production system is essentially a success of changing fossil fuels into food. So, raising energy prices are almost higher food costs and even shortage for fossil fuels energy. If one day, one kind of discovered secondary man-made renew used energy can supply to any restaurants or homes to be used to cook at the cheap price, then the profit is very high for this kind of food production energy. Thus, future food production secondary energy consumption market is large and because the primary energy inputs for agriculture are higher than the energy outputs of the food. However, future secondary man-made renew used energy for food production system is only one part of whole energy consumer in food industry. The food production is related to whole food consumption market which includes: household cooking energy market, agriculture or vegetable, rice, fruit etc. foods farming machines energy market, food manufacturing factories market, food machine package market, transportation food delivery market, supermarket or fruit/food sale stores market. They must need any energy inputs to achieve the food production or food transportation or warehouse / stores electricity supply or cooking energy needs. Hence, these food suppliers relate to any whole food factory manufacturers, food retailers, food wholesalers, farmers and home/restaurant cookers, all of them must need to use energy to carry on their food producing or food cooking or food transportation activities every day in overall food industry. Thus, it seems that undiscovered any second energy demand will be increased, when the primary energy supply number is decreasing. Also, when people can accept to use secondary energy to replace primary energy to be used for any cooking, transporting food, manufacturing food, food retail stores or warehouse food delivery energy need activities. Then, the secondary energy price will be fall down to attract many food energy consumers.